The Biscuit Tin Letters

Wartime Correspondence

by

William and Alice Lowries

Compiled by

Jane Watson

This book is published by

Lowres Publishing

First printed edition 2019
ISBN No 978–0–9957760–1-2

Contents

Introduction *Page 4*

Brian Lowries' Introduction *Page 7*

1941 *Page 14*

1942 *Page 39*

1943 *Page 74*

1944 *Page 116*

1945 *Page 171*

Maps of North Devon *Page 206*

Family background *Page 209*

Postscript *Page 220*

Introduction

Before my father died, he told me he had saved some letters written to him by his parents during the Second World War. He was not sure what to do with them and considered throwing them away. I asked him not to do that as I would like to read them. At the time I did not read them however. After my parents had both passed away, I found an old leather case which had once belonged to my mother and inside this were various family papers and letters, but not the ones my father had mentioned. It was several years later that I came across a biscuit tin and there inside, neatly labelled in brown envelopes, were the Wartime letters. Father had kept them after all.

The biscuit tin containing the letters in brown envelopes

The letters were all from my grandparents, both born in the last part of the Victorian period, describing their life in North Devon, and recounted how they managed during the Second World War. There were no letters from my father, Brian, the recipient of the letters, but in the leather case I found a note by him explaining why he had originally kept them. This is the second introduction to them, and his voice is heard. Also, in the leather case were a few letters from other family members, who are mentioned in the grandparent letters, and some of these have been included in the timeline.

The letters themselves mention little about the progress of the War; family and friends, unknown to us now come and go, the weather, growing vegetables and the hens are the main topics. The Ministry of Information produced posters which warned people not to discuss the war, and this, as well as the possibility that the letters might be read by the Censor (*letter July 27th '44)* may account for why little is written about it. Woolacombe beach was used from July 1943 as a practise area for the D Day landings; the letters just hint at this– "down below is a very busy place these days "(*Summer '43)* and in another letter "a good deal of gun fire goes on" (*Nov 1st '43*).

By 1941, the German blockade of shipping created food shortages. There were various initiatives to encourage people to grow their own food, become self- sufficient and experiment with the produce that they did have. This was presented as "The Kitchen Front", which encouraged civilians to take an active role in the fight against the Germans. This would account for the comment, through all the trials of the kitchen garden and the egg production, that Alice wrote in April 1942 "Hope I do not weary you with all this, but I would like to make a success of it". Brian had studied Horticulture at Wisley Horticultural College in the 1930s, and his mother, a keen gardener herself, often asked for his advice.

Many of the family photographs which I have inserted were taken in the 1940s, and were I believe, taken with a box Brownie camera. This was a very basic camera, which took black and white photographs, about 3ins by 2ins in size. I have occasionally cropped and if possible sharpened some of the pictures. However, the quality of the photographs remains variable, and they are just family snaps of the era.

The letters have been copied exactly; abbreviations and punctuations or the lack of them, have been left as written. I have not stated in advance who wrote each letter, but rather have left the style and tone of the writing to speak for itself. Alice (*Cambria font*) wrote in a conversational way, and William (*Calibri font*) in a more precise manner.

Finally, thank you to my family for their encouragement and suggestions.

Jane Watson (née Lowries)

October 2015

Brian Lowries' Introduction

My parents living in Devonshire during the War Years 1940 – 1945

Although War with Germany was declared in 1939, life went on as usual, with rationing being introduced gradually. It was termed a "phoney War". In 1941, however, the War was real with bombing of London and the big cities, causing great destruction and loss of life.

My parents decided to leave Buckinghamshire in 1940, moving to Devonshire, to Mortehoe. My mother spent part of her early life in Devonshire, attending a school in Bideford as a boarder; living with her mother and sister and brother on a farm, with her mother's second husband (*John Ridd)*, and his children. I believe she felt it was home, returning to the County.

Devonshire was well out of danger, the exception being Plymouth and the Dockland. The Army and American Forces were much in evidence on land off (sic) the coast. The Home Guard too was getting organised slowly in the District, as elsewhere.

The parents were keen to make a start growing food in the way of vegetables, but they were up against adverse conditions, with the proximity of the coast, 2 ½ miles away, and facing Atlantic gales with much rain was no help. It was soon realised that in order to grow anything worthwhile steps had to be taken to provide some shelter for the garden. A gardener (Old Dadds) came regularly from Ilfracombe to help. He stripped off earth from their ground, which of course left the underlying soil even poorer than before, to build 5 ft. high turf walls on the seaward side of the ground. This did much to check the wind and to enable some quite useful crops to mature. A well-built teak greenhouse was purchased for tomato culture especially sited away from the strongest wind. Raspberries, strawberries, gooseberries and some apple trees were planted; the soft fruits bore reasonable crops according to the season and weather, and also the depredations of the slug population. My mother was always out with a tin collecting these pests, a never ending chore, as with the weeds, which grew apace in this wet climate – not withstanding the soil was then so poor, weeding it was necessary to keep up the fertility.

In 1941, the parents were approached by the Billeting Officer to ask them to take 2 young boy evacuees from London, 5 ½ & 9 years. They stayed for about 6 months. They had been billeted with a clergyman's widow in Woolacombe, a large house containing 3 ladies, a maid, a daily cook and other help – pleading illness for not keeping them! My mother found these two "toughs" a trial & tiring, with big appetites and the washing of their underclothes. The elder boy spent a good time with the local farmer, but the younger, who used disgusting words, swore & was disobedient, was a "little toad", with a charming smile. They finally left in the Autumn of that year.

In 1941, my mother proposed keeping some hens, but in order to do so, a chicken house, chick wire netting & posts to support it would be needed. Permits were required for building materials & particularly anything made of wood. Eventually, however, a firm of greenhouse and shed builders in London agreed to construct a hen house for £10, which would be despatched by train. Second hand sheds were scarce. I offered to set the posts in the ground, & in doing so inadvertently plunged the crow bar through a water pipe from their bungalow – some help! When all was ready, a hen with a sitting of 13 eggs was obtained locally; my father thought that 13 was an unlucky number to commence this activity! I believe that the 13 were actually reduced in number through illness & accidents, which commonly occurs with chicks. A constant egg supply was kept up throughout the War years & later, 40 a week at the peak. Letters from my mother describing the odd behaviour of the birds make amusing reading, interesting too & also at times frustrating. Later a beach hut was offered to my parents who needed additional space for the hens. This was purchased and delivered to them, but being heavy & cumbersome, it took several men to man handle it past the bungalow & the turf walls in the kitchen garden. Inside the hut were found some tents & other equipment, which the owner wanted to sell. The tents were disposed to local friends & members of the family.

My brother Ronald (Ron) could not use his Morris 8 car, because of the petrol rationing, so he asked at the outbreak of War if he could leave it with the parents for the duration & this being agreed, it was under cover in their garage raised off the wheels. Later, my brother drove it locally, but was not very keen to drive after a slight collision occurred, leaving their lane to enter the Wafar Road to Mortehoe from Woolacombe. Little damage was done to it – cost £5 to repair the car wing. As a sequel to this accident, the high bank at this junction was cut back by the Council, the farmer giving the land to my father helped pay some of the cost. Mother also drove the car around locally, with much trepidation & survived the ordeal with only one slight mishap.

My father, a Quantity Surveyor, travelled to London, occasionally to conduct some work there & he also received work by post for him to complete. My mother took an interest in local organisations as much as she was able, helping in the canteen run by B. (*presume this to be the British Restaurant organisation, which was set up to provide basic meals off- ration. These canteens were often run by older volunteer ladies as their contribution to the War effort)* She did an immense amount of work repairing & making small garments for a children's Nursery (Tiffen) quite near to them. Her old hand sewing machine, Frister & Rossmann did Yeoman service and in time new needles & bobbins were required, but were scarce, almost unobtainable, as the machine was German. I do not know how this was overcome.

Throughout the War years, despite rationing & shortages of certain items, life went on as usual; milk was delivered by a local farmer, the grocer called to take an order & to deliver, the postman came, the coal heating fuel was delivered, logs were obtainable & the Doctor not too far away. A local bus (Yeo's) would take one to Ilfracombe to visit the Dentist, Optician, or for the purchase of more important things.

Everyone in the country is concerned with the weather, & in Devonshire & especially on the coast, it affects the people who are permanent residents – heavy and constant rain delivered by storm clouds in the Atlantic is a trial. Buffeting salt laden winds cause considerable damage to tiles, fences etc. One night father's new tool shed disappeared over the hedge into the farmer's field. The salt in the air caused the metal windows in the bungalow to rust away, to be replaced with wood. Only certain shrubs will flourish under these conditions, notably Hydrangeas, Tamarisk, Escallonia, Tracantha (large glossy leaves), Fuchsias & Olearia, Hebes etc. Washing pegged to a clothes line was wrenched off in the wind, with corners taken off the clothes. Lovely sunny days did occur from time to time, but often on a sunny day in summer, a mist would suddenly appear off the sea, blotting out the coast line – an occurrence not believed at first by my father. Life in the countryside particularly in Wartime with shortages, restrictions imposed by the Authorities creates a regime of self reliance & some planning, & brings out the ability to do things oneself.

Down Top, Poole Lane, Woolacombe, North Devon, 1940

The teak greenhouse and plants being unpacked for the new garden, 1940

View from the bungalow towards Woolacombe beach and the Atlantic, 1940

(From July 1943 this beach was used by the Americans for practise landings for D Day.)

I regard my parents as excellent communicators keeping the members of the family in touch with each other (two brothers & sister with self). Their letters, written jointly for most of the time were lucid & models of their kind. Ronald and myself were in reserved occupations & therefore not subject to service in the Armed Forces. Bob was in the Army, first of all in transport instructing women to drive, later transferring to the War Dogs branch. Phyllis joined the W.A.A.F. in the ranks, later obtaining a Commission. Her postings seemed continuous, my father notifying me & other members of our family of her address, if it was not secret.

Other news which was passed around, concerned relations, mainly my mother's sister, Lily, nieces, Dorothy, Lillian, Devonshire relatives by marriage of the Ridd family living & farming in North Devon. Bob did not see his parents for four years, as he was abroad for part of the time. My brother Ron & I made our way to visit and stay when we could, during the holidays. Both of us brought our respective fiancées to see the parents, & they were received and made very welcome, as newcomers to the family. In 1944, my mother travelled to Wiltshire for my marriage to Betty Butler, but my father did not feel that he could manage the journey in Wartime.

Brian Lowries in the 1930s

1941

Down Top

Poole Lane

Woolacombe

N.Devon

August 8 .41

My dear Brian,

Many happy returns of your birthday on Monday, we are sorry to send only socks, but am sure you can always do with them. If they are not large enough send them back some time & I will get you some more. We have not been to the shops so these are some I bought Daddy in Barnstaple all I could get then & not really his color.

We sent to Bravingtons to ask if they had a suitable watch & all they said was that they had solid gold watches from 5 guineas. Our idea was to give you a watch which you could always wear. I know I've seen them advertised to withstand dust and wet, but it's wartime & everything is different, so in despair we turn to socks again.

Would you like any knitted thing for Home Guard duty for cold nights, helmet etc. I could knit that with pleasure if you say what you want.

Phyllis surprised us with a letter on Tuesday morning, the first since we saw her to say she was being posted to Bideford & would come home first; which she did in the afternoon & stayed the night.

In the excitement of change etc she may forget your birthday, her address is now

Northam House

Northam

Nr. Bideford.

She is billeted with 2 other girls & has a bedroom to herself & a sitting room between them, it's super ! she says. It's quite a new station, they are the first girls to arrive there & only one other W.A.A.F. corporal so she will have some responsibility we gather.

Phyllis stayed on Wednesday to meet a gathering of the Clans, for Bob & Dorothy were bringing over Fred Ridd & his wife to tea. They had picnic lunch at Mortehoe after which Fred and his wife visited Auntie and Uncle who eventually drove them up here but did not stop whilst Dorothy & John walked up & Bob and David stayed behind to bathe.

Auntie Lucy came back later & took Phyllis to the X roads to get the bus to Bideford, which goes right through.

Auntie Lily was unfortunately otherwise engaged, you can imagine it was a partying to tea without the two toughs who had their dinners in the kitchen. We have not heard anymore about getting them removed, so Daddy wrote to Miss Roberts yesterday. They start their holidays next week 15th. Derek never stays long at the farm now. I fancy the farmer gets fed up with him – I don't know.

Mr.Pile, farmer & billeting officer said that they never intended leaving the boys here all the winter, taking sandwich lunch & so on, but Miss Roberts did not say that. Pat Ferrars is coming on the 15th. We shall suggest that she stays a fortnight & goes back with Ronald who can only have a week.

I am just beginning to gather tomatoes as they color & bring them in to finish & I have collected over 1 lb that way already. Am keeping an account of every ounce!

The fish woman & farmer want to know when I will sell some! I shall bottle a few when they are more plentiful. I have bottled 4 jars of raspberries & made a little syrup for winter drinks but they are finished now. Phyllis had her first taste of peas here & we still have a few to come, they have been most enjoyable & worth while. The boys next door have passed the entrance exam for City of London School which is now at Marlboro' so they will be going in September.

Well Brian, I think mother has given you all the news. I wonder if you applied for that post at West Norfolk ?

I am much the same – only the head noises have returned recently. I am only taking <u>half</u> the medicine now, perhaps I shall have to go back to the original doses.

The weather has been variable.

Bank holiday was <u>very wet</u> since then fine. & wet again today (Friday) – one day we had terrific winds which blew raspberries off & buried the leaves of the runner beans. Ronald is coming for the last week of this month.

Phyllis is hoping to get home about once a week to stay one night.

Hoping you are well.

With love Yr affec father

W J. Lowries

The "toughs" were evacuee boys. The evacuation of children from the "Blitz" in large cities had begun on 1st September 1939.

Brian was a member of the Local Defence Volunteers, which was renamed the Home Guard in July 1940. The Home Guard consisted of men aged from 17 to 65 who were in reserved occupations, and not in the regular army. They were trained to defend the country in the event of invasion.

Brian in the L.D.V. (Local Defence Volunteers) Castle Howard School, Malton, Yorkshire

Food rationing began on 8th January 1940, and was finally abolished in 1954, when meat restrictions were lifted.

Clothes coupons were introduced in March 1940.

Petrol rationing was imposed in 1939, and ended in May1950

In June 1941 Germany had invaded Russia.

Letter from Brian's brother Ronald

49 Sheridan Rd
Worthing
Sx
8/8/41

Dear Brian

This is to wish you many happy returns of the 11th. I hope the enclosed will be acceptable. The writers are truly remarkable women – one was at Worthing last year and I heard her ~~spoke~~ speak. (pardon!)

I am afraid it is difficult to do much about presents these days so it seems to be limited to books.

I was glad to hear that you were able to get home for a break & have heard little bits of news from various sources. I had to go to London with one of the partners on bomb damage recently & having an hour to spare I called into see Mr. Shepherd*. He told me he had been down to Devon recently & had seen you & Phyllis.

I had a letter from home recently which told me of your trip to Salcombe. It must have been a welcome change for mother and Daddy. I suppose you went over to where Phyllis is stationed at Prawle?

Things continue here very much as usual & we have been very quiet from an air raid point of view.

The garden here has well re-payed the work that has been put into it & we have been very glad to have our own vegetables from the plot.

I expect you are kept busy with the work & no doubt you have done well with "toms". They are plentiful here, as of course, there is quite a sizable industry here in that line. Quite a few of the local bombs have affected glasshouses & I have had the job of counting hundreds of squares of glass.

There are some nurseries where they grow mushrooms & the owner took me round. It was very interesting to see them growing indoors.

Now Brian, I don't often preach to you but sometimes I feel I ought. You know what I believe & you know what I believe is the consequence of not being a Christian - A life without God. Can you face that without fear? or do you try to still the voice of God or to persuade yourself that it isn't true.

I wish you would read the Bible – fairly & with a seeking spirit. I believe it to be God's message to a needy world. Why not try by starting with a Gospel say St. Marks – the shortest! Read a chapter a day. I am sure you will never regret it.

I hope you are keeping well.

All best wishes

Your affec bro,

Ronald

** Mr.Shepherd had been a Quantity Surveyor colleague of William, and is mentioned occasionally in the letters.*

Letter from Aunty Lily – older sister of Brian's mother and frequent visitor to "Down Top".

Monterey

8 Apsley Terrace

Ilfracombe

Aug. 24th 1941

My dear Brian,

How good of you to send me such a lovely lot of tomatoes they are a treat. Mine are still very green - yours are lovely & packed beautifully, none in the shops.

I have been staying with Dorothy at the farm for a week & returned on Thursday because Bob was coming for a long weekend – then I go there again on Thursday I suppose for another week. David is going to stay with one of his school mates for a week on Wednesday at Bournemouth where the parents are staying, make a change for him.

I went over to "Down top" on Friday your mother's Birthday & when I got back here your parcel waiting. Then I went over yesterday & took charge while they all went to see Dorothy & have tea.

I want your Father & Mother to go & see Bobby in Hereford (a safe place) & get a change. I will look after the boys if they are still there. I think a change would do them both good & before the winter comes in September we might have some nice weather – we shall deserve it – yesterday was dreadful – in fact it seemed rain all the time.

Ronald looked very well – Pat has grown a big girl – I saw Fred Ridds two girls & his eldest boy – tall & very like John Ridd a nice fellow I should say, also his girls looked nice, they came to tea at Dorothys – I must try & see Fred's wife when I go to Dorothy again but it is about 5 ½ miles to walk there. They have bought a car but the boy & one girl are only beginning to learn to drive.

Once more thanking you very much for your kindness & with kindest love from your

Affectionate

Auntie Lily.

Down Top

Poole Lane

Woolacombe

N.Devon

August 27th 1941

Dear Brian,

I am writing for mother to acknowledge your letter on her birthday & P.O. (*postal order*) for rock plants also for the tomatoes which arrived safely. Mother will be writing next week when she has more time. At the moment, Ronald is here and Pat Ferrars – also two toughs & Phyllis comes over from Bideford about every 4 days.

Since your letter arrived, we went to see Dorothy at Swimbridge on Saturday, Phyllis came on Sunday, we drove her back on Monday to Bideford, went to Westward Ho to tea – back in evening. Tuesday picnic tea at Rockham & so the days pass. The want of petrol rather restricts our movements, but we get as many runs as we can in fine weather. The weather has improved somewhat but we have had no settled fine weather for about a month now.

As regards tomatoes, we have been very lucky. You sent a nice lot. Ronald bought a basket from Worthing & besides we have our own in the greenhouse which are ripening slowly. Our runner beans are full of flower but very few beans so far. If we should have a fine September no doubt we shall have plenty. Marrows are doing well.

The evacuees are still with us – this is their second weeks holiday, they return to school on Monday. Ronald also returns on that day.

As regards myself I am about the same. I have to continue the same treatment & see the Dr. in a months time. Mother is pretty well but very tired.

Your affec father

W J Lowries

Post card written by Ronald to Brian 27th August 1941, the same day as the previous letter. There is no stamp and possibly was included with this letter.

Bideford North Devon 1940s

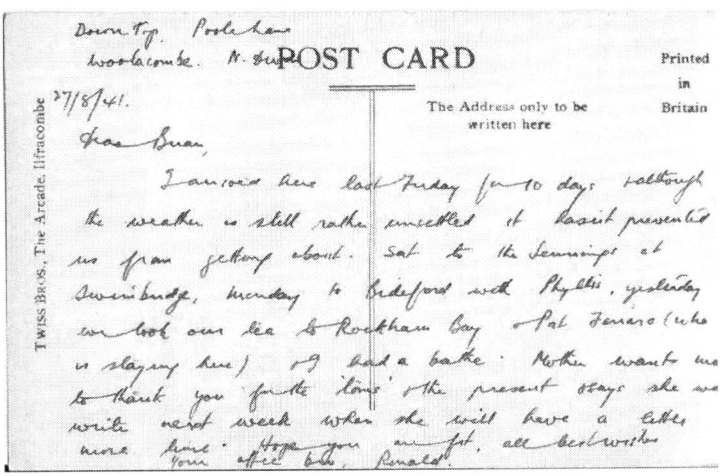

Down Top. Poole Lane
Woolacombe. N. [illegible]

POST CARD

Printed in Britain

The Address only to be written here

TWISS BROS., The Arcade, Ilfracombe

27/8/41.

Dear Brian,

I arrived here last Friday for 10 days & although the weather is still rather unsettled it hasn't prevented us from getting about. Sat to the [illegible] at Swimbridge, Monday to Bideford with Phyllis, yesterday we took our tea to Rockham Bay & Pat Ferraro (who is staying here) & I had a bathe. Mother wants me to thank you for the 'loan' & the present & says she will write next week when she will have a little more time. Hope you are fit, all best wishes

Your affec. bro, Ronald.

Post card written by Ronald Lowries

Transcript of the above postcard.

Down Top, Poole Lane

Woolacombe

27/8/41

Dear Brian,

I arrived here last Friday for 10 days & although the weather is still rather unsettled it hasn't prevented us from getting about. Sat to the Jennings at Swimbridge, Monday to Bideford with Phyllis, yesterday we took our tea to Rockham Bay & Pat Ferrers (who is staying here) & I had a bathe. Mother wants me to thank you for the "toms" & the present & says she will write next week when she will have a little more time. Hope you are fit. All best wishes.

Your affec bro, Ronald

Brian left Yorkshire in September 1941 and went to work in Winchester

Down Top

Poole Lane

Woolacombe

N.Devon

Oct 10th 1941

Dear Brian,

Thanks for your letter. We were very interested in your news.

No doubt taking up a new position is rather worrying until you feel your feet. Will take a week or two probably.

As regards a banking account you will have to open a "current" account. The N. Provincial Bank will do as I bank there at Ilfracombe. You will require an introduction (not guarantee) from a customer of the Bank which I can give you. I am writing to the Bank manager at Ilfracombe asking him to introduce you to the Branch Bank at Winchester.

It is usual to keep a balance of about £50 & of course you do not get any interest on current accs, as the interest is set against the cost of keeping your acc, clearing your cheques etc.

You should draw say £50 from the P.O. Savings Bank (in large notes say five £10 notes) call at the Bank one day between 10 & 2 & say that you wish to open an Account & that I have already introduced you from Ilfracombe. You will have to sign your usual signature (the one you will use in signing cheques) – You will require a cheque book – paying in book & a pass book. The cheque book can consist of "open" cheques or "crossed"cheques. I find the "open" cheques the better as you can then write yourself a cheque & get the money over the counter at any time. In writing a cheque to yourself say Pay "Self" and endorse the cheque on the back with your name. I enclose one of my old cheques to show you, and you needn't return it as it is of no value now. I hope this is all as clear as mud.

We had a rather tedious journey home – quite a job to get a seat in the train at Hereford – which came from Liverpool & was going to Plymouth, arrived home about 9.45pm.

Phyllis went by bus to Worcester & we heard from her this morning that she is enjoying herself.

Mother seems better for the change and I also.

We heard from Uncle Ernest that Kathleen has a baby daughter!

With love from us Both

Your affec father

W J Lowries

On October 2nd Germany attacked Moscow

Down Top
Poole Lane
Woolacombe
N.Devon

Oct 28th 1941

Dear Brian

Very many thanks for your letter on my 70th birthday and your kind wishes.

I received letters also from Ronald and Bobby and Phyllis phoned – also some books from Phyllis- one rather unique one.

We celebrated the event on Sunday here with Auntie Lily & Lillian (who is staying at Ilfracombe for a few days) and Lucy and Uncle Sidney. Mother and I also went yesterday (the 27th) to Ilfracombe, had lunch out at South Combes and tea with Aunt Lily and Lillian.

As regards the journey here, I quite agree that it is too long for a car. Anyway N. Devon is not very accessible and I suppose it was not very considerate of us to retire to such a spot when the rest of you are within a reasonable distance of London - of course if any of the family had been living with us at home at Chalfont we shouldn't have done so.

Mr Yeo (the builder) has now completed the stone walling at the entrance to our abode which I think is a great improvement. He is next going to make a concrete "workdown" outside the garage with a gully in the centre. This part of the drive has always been wet & soft & I think concrete is the only remedy.

We are glad you like your present address & are likely to stay. Sorry about the car being out in the weather. I suppose you cannot borrow a tarpaulin or some other covering? What about anti-freezing mixture – or will you have to empty the radiator?

It is rather depressing to try to advise people on gardening when the soil is so poor, and natural manures so difficult to obtain.

It is nice to find the staff friendly and helpful. I expect in the course of a few months you will know Hampshire as well or better than any county. You remember I have a little cottage in the New Forest near Lyndhurst a village called Woodlands,* not so very far from Southampton.

We are very sorry you have a cold and hope it will soon be better. Fancy Hampshire being colder than Yorkshire!

With love from mother

& Your affec father

W J Lowries

William must have inherited this cottage as Brian mentioned it in his memoir. In a later letter of 8th March 1944, William wonders why his (step) grandmother bought the cottage, as "it is not a very nice one".

Down Top

Poole Lane

Woolacombe

N.Devon

November 16 – 41

My dear Brian,

We were very glad to get your letter & interested to hear how you are getting on with your new job.

Thank you very much for sending on the recipes. I have been using up the tomatoes, green & otherwise, but I shall be very glad of the recipes for next year. I have pulped quite a lot of ripe tomatoes & have several jars of whole ones, have made blackberry syrup & elder wine & chutney from green tomatoes, as have quite a good store.

You are fortunate to live with people who will take the trouble to cook & experiment these days, tho' it's a bit awkward if one doesn't like some of the dishes when they've probably taken a good deal of preparing & used valuable articles.

Auntie Lily likes making her own cakes & does us as well you know, but we both get awfully short of fats & anxiously looking forward to the increased ration. Aunty Lucy sometimes gives us each some margarine as she buys her ration but does not make cakes.

Glad to hear you & Ronald were able to meet & had such a nice afternoon together. We are looking forward very much to having you both home for Christmas, have been making the pudding mixture & hope to boil it tomorrow, getting forward with preparations, one never knows what hindrances there will be, also I had to hurry because elder wine needs raisins so I used all I had & added sultanas to make up the amount, then the wine is strained & I kept the fruit to add to the Christmas pudding mixture.

Monday morning. Such a gale blowing all night, & still as bad this morning with sharp hail while our coal was being delivered. It doesn't do to look out of the window & see the shrubs etc. being blown almost out of the ground.

Outside the dining room at the corner where our little hedge fades away I planted some sturdy escallonias we had over, but they are almost out of the ground.

It's interesting to hear about the Reading people, will you ask the maiden name of the one who knew Phyllis & was a Georges student. (*Phyllis had been a student at St. Georges Hall, Reading University*). Phyllis will no doubt remember her. I think she was right about Greenham but don't think Phyllis writes to her now, she shared with Vera Grant afterwards & still very friendly with her. We've not seen Phyllis lately, sometimes she comes home often & rings up occasionally so we must ring her, only we don't know her off duty hours.

Did we tell you she has been before one Board for a Commission, the next step is a Board in London, much stiffer.

I hope you like your new district & find better soil there in more ways than one.

I will enclose a recent letter from Bobby & will send yours to him, he will be glad to hear your news.

Bobby was a driver in the Royal Artillery Regiment, stationed in Herefordshire.

Harry Watkins wrote a Circular letter which arrived recently to his wife & which she sends on to Auntie Lily who brings it for us to read & then on to Dorothy & Lillian & round to Betty's family. It was very interesting, typed from the desert it seems, a tent cover stretched between lorries, he enquired after everybody.

I hope you like the Home Guard members, did you have to give in your uniform when you resigned in Yorkshire?

With much love & hope your cold is better & that you are getting used to the southern air.

Yours ever affectionately

Mother

The following is a newspaper cutting saved by Brian, date unknown, of the obituary of Harry Watkins, the son of Aunty Lily. This shed light on what he was actually doing at the time his family received the circular letter mentioned in the letter of 16th November 1941.The battle of Bardia took place in early January 1942.

Soldier who became Devon farmer dies

BRIG. HARRY R. B. WATKINS, of The Croft, Dunchideock, near Exeter, who won the D.S.O. at the relief of Tobruk and scored a brilliant personal success at the second battle of Bardia, has died at his home at the age of 70.

He joined the Army in 1914, was commissioned in 1916, and served in the Royal Tank Regiment from its formation in 1916 to his retirement in 1948.

He fought in the Western Desert in Libya for two years. At Bardia he commanded a mixed force of Britons and South Africans which made a night attack from the flank of the port, previously thought almost impregnable. Bardia was overrun, a large number of German and Italian prisoners were taken, and the Allied forces suffered hardly any casualties.

BECAME A FARMER

Brig. Watkins farmed at Dunchideock from his retirement to his death. He was chairman of the horticultural section of Devon Farmers' Union, a member of the N.F.U. National Fruitgrowers' Council, chairman of the West-country Growers' Association, chairman of the Save the Children fund at Exeter, and a prominent worker for the church.

He leaves a widow and one son, Lt.-Col. Bryan Watkins, of the Royal Tank Regiment.

Obituary notice of Harry Watkins

The North African Campaign lasted from June 1940 to May 1943. The later letter of 12th July 1943 stated that he had to go to North Africa again, and according to the letter 30th November 1944 his future job was to be in occupied Germany. An internet search revealed his name to be Major General Harry Reginald Bristow Watkins, born 1894.

Aunty Lily's son, Harry Reginald Bristow Watkins as a young man in the Royal Tank Regiment.

Down Top

Poole Lane

Woolacombe

N.Devon

Dec 12th 1941

Dear Brian,

This is in reply to your letter of 27th Nov for which we thank you.

You appear to have settled down to your new job – but we do not gather whether you really like it. I hope so. We are very interested in your account of your doings.

We heard from Ronald yesterday that he and you met at Chicester again & had another fine afternoon. Very lucky. The weather here lately has been very mild & wet & stormy; but so long as the ice & snow keep away the winter will seem shorter.

We hope your H.G. practises with live hand grenades went off without any hitch. Is Ronald joining the H.G?

Phyllis went to London about a fortnight ago to go before another Board & if accepted expected to go to Swanage for her training course of several weeks. We have been expecting to hear every day. She doesn't think in the circumstances that she will be home for Xmas. Ronald thinks of coming on the Wednesday & returning the following Monday.

As regards your question about bringing a cake, mother would like one, not "madeira" – chocolate if one is to be had in these times. You said you were bringing a couple of Cyclemen – I told mother you were bringing two cyclists for Xmas. Afterwards I found it was Cyclamen. Quite a different matter!

Yes, Harry is in the fighting in Libya. His wife received a cable recently that he was all right. I expect you rather enjoy your fire watching night – especially the fish & potatoes & jam tarts.

I am afraid that the Japanese coming into the War will make it much longer – the whole world is now practically at War. What a blot on modern civilisation and the teachings of all the religious sects including Christianity.

We presume that you will be catching a train on the 24th which is due at Mortehoe at 9pm. I am afraid that mother will not be meeting you in the car as she doesn't like night time driving.

Love from us both.

Also Auntie Lily who is here today.

Your affec father

W J Lowries

December 7th The Japanese attacked the American Pacific Fleet at Pearl Harbour.

December 8th Britain and America declared war on Japan.

December 11th Germany declared war on America.

1942

Down Top

Poole Lane

Woolacombe

N.Devon

Jan. 14 – 42

My dear Brian,

Thank you very much for your nice long letter also the Gardening Booklet, which should be a great help, it's so well illustrated, thanks very much for it.

I would be glad if when you are ordering your seeds you could get sufficient for us at the same time, $^{1}/_{2}$ an ounce each of various greens should be enough don't you think. Dadds (*gardener*) usually grows too much of everything & it's such waste. Toogoods will be better, for we made several sowings last year, of onions & carrots & nothing appeared at all & Dadds said it happened at other places he works.

I am thinking more seriously about having a few fowls, so if you can find me a leaflet with any guidance I shall be glad. I believe I shall have to apply to the War Agriculture Committee in Barnstaple for (a) permit to buy meal.

Talking to Mr. Norman yesterday who was down putting me up an end shelf in the greenhouse, he could probably let me have some young chicks, he rears his own, then I shall want a house. One or two people have been buying bathing huts from Woolacombe for this purpose. I must enquire about them.

Glad you found out the trouble with the car, thanks for the tip. We have 4 new plugs for ours now which Ronald paid for when he was home. I am keeping the little lamp going underneath these days, we have had an occasional sharp frost.

Phyllis was home again last Tuesday, just as we were preparing to go into Combe to lunch so she came with us. She had not heard anymore, she may be home again this week the washing she left behind, there is no convenience at her billet for such things & afraid to send to laundry whilst so uncertain how much longer she will be there.

Your H.G. instruction certainly sounds pretty gruesome, but after reading the atrocities committed by the Germans in Russia printed in full in the "Sunday Dispatch" they should certainly have a taste of their own medicine, they were just the same in the last war & it was all overlooked afterwards, they don't understand ordinary decent behaviour.

I hope you enjoyed the party last Saturday, expect you were not sorry to escape the Yorkshire one this time, by the way, if you should want such a thing, I believe I have your dress suit or Daddy's could be altered to fit you & no coupons needed, you might bear it in mind.

Could you order me also some dwarf stock seeds you were telling me about. We have broad bean & Valencia onion seed bought in Hereford.The orchids are still fairly good so have not thrown them away yet, also Ronald's white chrysants are still lasting.

Hope you did not spill the wine going home. Auntie Lily was very pleased with her Cyclamen, said she had always admired and wanted one, mine is flourishing with lots more buds.

Must stop now for post; hope the seeds will not be a bother to you.

With much love and hope you keep well in spite of cold nights on duty.

Yours ever affectionately

Mother

Down Top

Poole Lane

Woolacombe

N.Devon

February 5 – 42

My dear Brian,

Thank you very much for your informative letter & the leaflets since. I did not reply sooner hoping to hear some news of a fowl house, but nothing has come of enquiries through various people.

I wrote to Plymouth for a permit for timber, the address given me by a merchant in Braunton who is willing to make the house if he can get the timber, & after keeping me waiting a week the Ministry of Supply tell me that I must first get a Certificate to Purchase such timber from the Ministry of Agriculture & Fisheries authorising the use of such timber. And we sneer at the Germans & their controls. However, I had already written to Whites of Bromley, who made the greenhouse & they have given me an estimate to make a 7ft x 5ft x 5ft 6ins, a Front with $^5/_8$ th matching for £10, & we have accepted that.

It will take 2 or 3 weeks to make & then a certain delay on the railway. We only accepted the estimate yesterday as we were waiting to hear news of 2nd hand houses.

We had a card from Phylllis yesterday to say they were sitting for a written exam all day today & travelling to Stanmore tomorrow Friday. It sounds a terribly gruelling Course at Swanage 3 weeks intensive, 5 girls.

Mr. Dadds came yesterday for the first time for weeks but has not turned up today. It's very cold but fine, he has a rupture & so will have to be careful not to do anything too ----- *missing*

Phyllis Lowries 1942

During the War Phyllis was a War Substantive Officer in the Women's Auxilary Air Force.

Down Top
Poole Lane
Woolacombe
N.Devon

March 20 -42

My dear Brian,

The parcel of seeds arrived yesterday perfectly packed. It's a most exciting parcel & thank you for all the trouble you have taken & thought in selection.

Mr. Dadds was here on Wednesday, but had to go early because of a heavy cold developing & he felt rotten. A thick cold mist came over in the afternoon, which often happens here, it persisted all yesterday until about 3. oc. when the best of the day was lovely & I did some clearing up in the garden in the evening.

Dadds has not been very much this year, he is no weather prophet & often stays away & we have a lovely day. I think he has plenty of work in Combe. We bought some Broad Beans in Hereford last year & they have been in some time so Daddy says. I ought to send these back to you, so what do you suggest. You have probably lost my letter, but I did say that we had them, or are you thinking of the fowls, or is it advisable to save them & plant them in the Autumn for next year.

The cucumber I wanted for the frame to grow on a hot bed, will these ridge ones do in there?

You must let us know how much we owe you for all these seeds, or we can't ask you to get us anything again.

The ground is very sticky still so our planting will be late. I believe we usually are for one reason or another. Our potatoes are still holding out well & are very good in color & flavour.

Phyllis was home last week for 7 days. She did not get through the exam & is now on the E. coast. Her address is now: -

897081 Cpl. Lowries P.U.

W.A.A.F.

R>A>F> Stoke Holy Cross

Near Norwich

Norfolk

She didn't have a very good reception from the C.O. because she had pipped her exams I suppose, but she thinks she will like it there & get good experience. The station prides itself on it's efficiency.

How is the young fellow who was injured in the H.G. exercises, most unfortunate & the man who fired at him must be feeling terrible about it.

You do not say how your cold is, but hope you are feeling better & will soon shake it off completely if the weather gets better. Today is lovely. Aunty Lily is here, she usually stays the night & we go into Combe to the B.R. together in the morning. *(The British Restaurant – Volunteer non - profit making organisation, set up in Wartime, to provide basic inexpensive meals for those in need).*

I don't see the Lucerne amongst the seeds, had you forgotten it or not able to get it? Aunt Lily sends her love & thanks you for seeds, she has already sown some peas & shallots, the latter from hers of last year. I hope the sunflowers will do well, we shall look gay. I shall buy & put in the shallots myself as Dadds may not be here & the ground is ready for them.

Will write again later. Did I tell you the fowl house had arrived over a week ago & looks very good but as it must be bolted down I am still waiting for Mr. Norman to come & fix it, he is very busy & short handed, but said he would do it one evening if he couldn't find any other time, but it's wearisome having to wait for everything so long, makes one wish never to have started on it. I'm also waiting for a permit for wire netting, they told me that it had all been allocated for the last quarter, no more until March 15th but I hear nothing.

Much love & hope you are better, our love & many thanks.

Yours ever affectionately

Mother

Will in his dressing gown, and Mr. Dadds later in 1948

February 15th Singapore surrendered to the Japanese on 'Black Sunday'.

February 19th 135 Japanese planes attacked Darwin in northern Australia. 240 people were killed and 10 wounded.

March 8th Dutch East Indies surrendered unconditionally.

March 20th Germany's all-out aerial assault on Malta started.

Down Top

Poole Lane

Woolacombe

N.Devon

Thursday April 2nd / 42

Dear Brian,

We had been wondering if you would be able to come home for Easter, but as we haven't heard anything we presume that you are unable to get away.

We were very glad of the seeds you sent us a short time ago, but you must let us pay for them. Old Dadds was here last week on a fine day, and many seeds were sown, and now we have had a good deal of rain only it is very cold yet. We were sorry about the misunderstanding about the broad beans & cucumbers. I suggested sending back the broad beans as I thought in your position you could make use of them better than we could, but I suppose we could keep them by us for another year.

Mother would like some indoor cucumber seeds – the ridge variety didn't do very well last year – also some leek seeds. We cannot get the latter in this District. As regards maize – is any special cultivation necessary? We cannot find anything about it in our wonderful gardening books.

We expect to be lonelier than usual this Easter. Ronald cannot come & Phyllis is in Norfolk. Do you know her address? It is ---- *as in previous letter*

Mother has started keeping fowls – the fowl house is up – have just secured the permit for wire netting – and a hen is busy sitting on 13 eggs – a very unlucky number I think.

I wonder if the end of the basic ration of petrol will affect you very much. We do not know if we shall have to "put up" the car at the end of June, but think we probably shall. I see a suggestion of the Government taking over the tyres of all cars "put up". That would settle it for us without a doubt.

With our love

Your affec father

WJL

Cars were jacked up and put on blocks if not in use, as they could not be left standing on the type of tyres used at the time.

Down Top

Poole Lane

Woolacombe

N.Devon

April 13 – 42

My dear Brian,

Just a line to hope that you are now feeling better & have had Doctor's advice.

If it is liver & a chill you want some special medicine so don't hesitate. I had just gone to bed when you rang & came down but couldn't get hold of the phone, expect you had had to wait about some time to get thro'. If you don't feel well enough for the journey can you put it off for the week, it wouldn't make any difference to us & we are not likely to go away.

Tell Mr. Shepherd not to give you rations for the weekend, a week is a different matter. Phyllis never used to bring anything except for official leave & we can manage.

Next Monday one lot of eggs are due to hatch & I am getting worried in case the hen who should be sitting on them gets fidgety & wish I could think of somewhere to move the first lot to. Our wire netting is not up yet & hardly likely to be as the builder's boy joins up on Thursday & they have no help now.

Our piano has gone today to a sale room in Ilfracombe & will be put up on Wed, prices fetch fantastic figures here just now, so we thought a good time to get rid of it. I have just written to Mrs.

Collins offering her all your old music for her pupils if she likes to have it.

If we don't hear again we shall expect you on Sat. afternoon, if you can come Friday & have an extra day or two we shall be delighted.

Much love hoping you are on the mend

Yours ever affectionately,

Mother

Down Top

Poole Lane

Woolacombe

N.Devon

April 42

My dear Brian,

Thank you very much for your two letters & cucumber seeds in the first (which I have planted) & this weeks packet of Leeks & the parsnips with the extraordinary name, many thanks for all.

Mr. Dadds was here on Wed & cleared some ground & planted potatoes, then yesterday we had an awful day of gales & rain, could hardly stand up to it, so we were glad he did not come. This morning, wishing this whilst drinking my early tea, looks lovely, sun shining, but Baggy still leafing. (?) You and Mr. Keller have been busy to raise & send off so many onion plants & looking after so many gardens & allotments, it sounds a full time job with fire watching thrown in on top of H.G. Glad to hear you have won your stripe.

After worrying you for the Leek seed, old Dadds gently said that he has written to his son in Bridgwater for some & had got ¼ ounce, so will plant your seeds here & perhaps be glad later of a few plants if these do well !

We shall look forward very greatly to your weekend or longer, before our petrol gives out. I hope we have about ½ full now & 2 (*gallons*) to come this month.

We didn't really expect you at Easter knowing you must have so much to do, & the weather has been horrible. Auntie Lily came & spent it here the week before Lillian was with her for the weekend only.

Thank you for all the information about chick food. I will write it out, please thank Mr. Shepherd for his hints. I have 2 sitting hens now & left them both free, there is a week between acquiring them. Mr. Norman said they would be all right, but they had a scrap one night & I found they had changed places, so the new hen is sitting on eggs a week old & I had 3 eggs broken in the new nest; pushed away on one side matted in hay. I've left them – hens –as they were & now shut one up & leave the other free turn & turn about. What we do in our ignorance!

I shouldn't bother about the Lucerne *(packet of seeds)* we shan't have any too much room after having several extra things this year, unless of course you have already got it.

I think I must have told you that the pullets I ordered turned out to be cockerels, that is what the poultry man wrote me but he had not enough to go round & I had only ordered 6 over the phone without writing to confirm it.

I saw Miss Woollard in the week & she was full of advice about these hens & what I ought to do, they, the hens I mean seem worrying things to look after & Miss W. whose parents keep poultry & ducks, she herself keeps ducks, they are the Woolacombe Weaver people & have a loom on the way down to Woolacombe. I ought she says to lift them off the nest sprinkle the eggs, puff insect powder into the hen's feathers & I don't know what. We have the wire netting & Mr. Yeo has promised to come & put it up for us & bring some poles with him, so we have no run for them yet.

Daddy is making the dog box into a coop & Uncle Sidney has made the run for it; for the chicks, if & when they arrive. So many things one needs to know in the initial stages seems to me. The first chicks are due by the 20th.

Hope I do not weary you with all this but I would like to make a success of it.

With much love & looking forward to seeing you.

Yours ever affectionately

Mother

Down Top

Poole Lane

Woolacombe

N.Devon

May 19 -42

My dear Brian,

I feel I have been owing you a letter for some time, but the days pass quickly & we have been back to cold & wet when it felt too cold to sit & write; some afternoons I go & have a lay down & there is no time. However after days of rain & fog it is sunny again in the dining room & one feels more like doing things.

I promised to let you know about the chicks, well the second brood hatched 7 out of 9 eggs, how she did it I don't know for during that time the gales were awful & the fowl house rocked backwards & forwards, it's not strong enough, & the wind whistled through the corner where she sat. I put the coop ready in the house & waited an opportunity to move the hen into it, but when the chicks were ready she marched them into it of her own accord out of the dirty nest; I thought it very clever of her. Each hen has a small enclosure with short stakes until we can get Mr. Norman along & the stakes which he has ordered. And we must have the house strengthened & when we shall get hold of him is a problem, everybody wanting him & no help to be had. The second hen has only 5 chicks now, one went off his feed the first week & was dead next morning, the other suddenly carried his head on one side, like a stiff neck & died on Sunday, nice size too, have wondered since if it could have been crop trouble, but there it is, the first hen soon lost one of hers in the first week & another was stunted, like a little hunchback, so we killed him, after giving him more than a fortnight, they certainly are chancy things, they certainly are good hens both of them. I have to watch Pushkin (*the cat*), he often stalks round them, & one chick got through the netting, so Daddy helped me to round it up. Just as I grabbed the chick, the old hen came sailing over the netting at me, afraid I dropped the chick over & then the hen had to be coaxed back without letting out all the chicks, it's a game.

Mr.Dadds has filled up the kitchen garden, almost every inch. You know how obstinate he is about new ideas to him, we gave him a selection of your leaflets & would you believe it, he of his own accord put grass cuttings from the drive on the compost heap & levelled it over, he usually regards it as my fancy bit of rubbish & does something else with his.

The tomatoes are coming along steadily, so far neither have shown signs of pegging out, so later on will put the small pot ones outside against the greenhouse in big boxes.

Ronald just had a letter from Bobby, he seems very fit & busy, also Ronald wrote in the week, he is very busy & becomes de-reserved on July 1st & is wondering what will happen to him then.

We are waiting to hear from Phyllis, she came safely through the Norwich raids & was sent to Swanage a week ago.

We don't think we will put in for petrol after June, the papers say that you must have a cast iron reason for wanting it.

Harry has been home 3 or 4 weeks & Auntie Lily spent a day with them at Bideford, she says that he looks just the same, but was sent home on sick leave & injured a rib on board ship, which was causing him some pain, he had an uneventful sea journey, no convoy.

I hope you have been quite well all this time, no doubt very busy with your various gardens, trust they are progressing satisfactorily & that you will try & avoid being blown up by fellow H.G.s. I see there was another explosion recently, several killed & injured, we shall lose our defenders before the offence begins if these things go on.

I hope Mrs. Shepherd is keeping well, you must tell me when the happy event is expected.

I wonder if you will get to see Jock this Whitsun as you hoped to do, if so remember me very kindly to them & hope Mrs. Jock & son are very well.

The garden is looking very nice, brooms are making a show this year & the birch is quite flourishing, apple trees are a mass of blossom & the black currants full of promise, also gooseberries but I haven't any sugar to play with this year, so must bottle if there are enough without.

Pushkin caught 3 baby rabbits early last week, from the Lawrence garden, one got in here, I don't know how, & any number of mice, but he hates windy & rainy days & doesn't know what to do with himself, then he gets rough & hurls himself from chair to chair, I don't enjoy this sort of thing.

With love from us both

Yours ever affectionately

Mother

P.S.

Had a nice letter from Dorothy recently. Mr. Denny is pretty well, manages a walk most days, no news of Frasers in her letter. I've had 2 letters recently from Blanche in Australia she had registered her name & wondered what sort of job if any, they will give her, she is far from strong, not fit for much.

How has Mr.Shepherd fared with his chicks, hope he has been successful with them. Our farmer spent 21/- s on day old chicks, some cockerels & the hen pecked them the second day & 3 died so he took them away & put them with a lamp & now has one left out of those. Out of a hatching he only got 2 chicks, then a hen stole her nest (as they say) & she has 11 chicks & they appear these 11 to be doing well.

Alice in the hen run, after the War, August 1948 – this hen house probably the beach hut.

Down Top

Poole Lane

Woolacombe

N.Devon

June 23 – 42

My dear Brian,

Thank you very much for the Pyrethrum Powder (*insecticide)* received yesterday, the bath salts & your several letters, it is most kind & thoughtful of you & I appreciate it very much. My feet are much better than they were when you were home. I have left off the elastic band with pad & no stockings & have used the salts 2 or 3 times & found great ease & benefit; so shall go on with them.

I got one packet of Radox from T.Whites (*chain of chemist shops*) but they seem scarce & came from behind the counter sort of!

I am glad to say the chick with a bad neck has recovered & growing, am sure old Pushkin got it & probably the hens attacked him for he skirts round there now rather nervously, so it's a blessing that it happened before I parted the chicks from the hens.

Both hens have started laying. I have had 5 eggs since the 16th – no eggs yesterday & on Sunday the old hen laid under the house. Ken Yeo put up a temporary partition to give the hens the house, then I found the big chicks always chasing the little ones & wouldn't let them eat; so I have one width of wire across the big piece again, separating the two lots & the little ones are doing well now nearly as big as the others, they each get into the coop at night. I still gaze at them trying to discover their sex. I was up at the Normans the other evening & they have got a mixed lot of fowls, from black to light. Our speckly ones are light brown in front & pure white behind, almost half & half & the white one has slight tinges of light brown on his wing.

Last night about 11.30 both gone to bed the phone went & Phyllis was calling up to say that she is being posted tomorrow 23rd to somewhere in Devon or Cornwall, they won't say where, she arrives & will then be told where to go, so we may be seeing her before long. A.S.O. means Assistant Section Officer, "the lowest of the low" she says.

I took Auntie Lily & Dorothy to the Village one evening whilst Daddy & I stopped by the Church. Dorothy bought pottery for presents & spent quite a good bit; whilst waiting there Mr.Yeo comes along & Daddy tells him about the pierced drain pipe, which has turned out to be our main sewer. The next day Mr. Yeo came along & repaired it by putting a half collar under & the other half over & cementing them, he thinks it would be alright. Now that same evening he put up the wire netting & has promised to bring a carpenter along & do the job properly, also strengthen the fowl house. Mr. Norman has not been near, Yeo has also promised some rubroid for the roof to make it water tight.

This morning I saw old hen under the house and later went to fetch the egg and couldn't see one, then felt round, under the corner came across 5, one still warm, so that's ten since the 16th. Young hen chivvies the old one so I suppose she goes there to get out of her way, but I have wired it off now, because it would be difficult to find them if she went further under, hope she does not go -----

The rest of the letter is missing.

June 7th The Siege of Sebastopol started in the Crimea

June 21st Tobruk captured by Rommel

No date or address for this letter. It was in a bundle for 1942 (The same writing paper & ink as June 23rd 1942)

My dear Brian,

Very many thanks for the Bay tree, it is a splendid looking tree nice & compact & I have removed a lilac in order to give it room. I do hope that request was not a very expensive one. I was thinking of something a few inches high, so please let us pay for this. The Echinops are also facing the kitchen window, we want something cheerful to look out on & that makes a very bright border with the sunflowers etc.

We ordered some Cox's apples from Lord Wilmer's Estate, advertised in the Telegraph & they came on Saturday, lovely fruit & beautifully packed. We have ordered some keeping cooking apples from Harris, where the fruit came from, they were not ready. We have a tremendous crop of onions, under the car at present, it is very dry there, but carrots will not be as good as last year, they got the fly before we noticed in time.

The maize has not matured, should I take it up & give the fowls just as it is, that is what I have done with barley & oats, & let them peck it, the sunflowers too are very slow to ripen, but of course the season has not been warm enough for these things & the winds have been almost continuous.

We had a lovely day yesterday & in the afternoon Mrs. Brown & I went down to Lee Lane & after floundering about in woods & bracken found a footpath which leads to Lee, then we turned back & hope to go direct next time.

Looking towards Lee, the Borough Valley, 1940

The village of Lee, August 1948

Are you likely to get your weekend soon, try & come Friday evening & return Monday, that makes it more worth the long journey. Phyllis left here by the last train on Thursday & did not arrive at her destination until Sunday lunchtime, she must have had enough of travel by that time, she took another suitcase with her, that large one of yours which you scarcely ever used.

Give Mrs. Shepherd my best wishes for herself & Susan Mary & hope that the young lady has settled down to home life & not keeping you all awake.

I have some honey from Mrs. Norman & hoping to get some more if she can spare it & thought if you come home you can take a pot back with you & I have one also for Ronald, but rather afraid to send it. I have risked it & sent one to Joan hoping it will be in time for Bobby's next leave which is about due. I packed it in a tin & hope it has travelled safely.

You sent us a very interesting description of camp life & we were glad that you had a good spell of weather, we thought of you.

Mr. Cary has just sent me a little rose tree rock variety – it must be Rosa Mulabilis (sic). I cannot find any description of it in my books, she says that it has flowered constantly with her. I have put it near the shed, but must find a better place for it in the rock garden. I have not replied & thanked her yet, nor for several remedies received from her some time ago for indigestion, but must write. I have been so busy cutting out & making little garments for the Twitchers Nursery, every week there is a fresh consignment which keeps me up to scratch. Mrs. Simon goes once a week with mending she has done for them & calls to see if I have anything ready to send, but I shall try & have a little time at weeding when the weather is suitable. I enjoy doing that as much as anything once I've got started & dressed for the part.

With much love & very many thanks for plants & hoping to see you before long.

Yours ever affec.   Mother

Monterey

8 Apsley House

Ifracombe

Aug.10th 1942

My dear Brian,

This is just a few lines to wish you "Many happy returns of your Birthday" & we will hope before another comes round this beastly War will be over. I went over to "Down top" yesterday afternoon & saw Ronald & his friend. Ronald looks very well & I found him doing the washing up after his dinner "Keeping his hands in"

he said. I am afraid the weather is not very promising for them so far, showers yesterday, & today it has not ceased so far. I believe they did get a good walk to Church & round Woolacombe way in the morning. This place is simply packed with visitors – I am sorry for them because I do think most people living in towns & at work all the year round need a change. I heard a number of people on Bank holiday had to return because they could not find places to board & when some did they were charged £1.00 a night, for only bed & breakfast. Some of these people here are a lot of thieves.

Harry is now in Scotland acting as "chief umpire" a temporary job – I am thankful he returned when he did from overseas. I ran across Bessie Curtis? the other day here, she tells me her boy Arthur wants to go into the Air Force but they can't spare him from the Farm.

Next paragraph damaged.

--- Your mother's garden is a blaze of color now & the kitchen garden in splendid order – my beans are very promising, also tomatoes coming along great at present – I have had about a doz lbs (*dozen pounds*) of peas – not bad for a tiny garden.

I expect you will get all news from home -are you getting any more holiday before Xmas. Lillian (*her daughter*) came here for a week with a friend & expects to get another long weekend from Torquay. I have also had Dorothy for 8 days – so although living in Devon, we do get visitors & not quite forgotten.

With all best wishes – good luck & good health

From your

Affectionate Auntie Lily

Down Top

Poole Lane

Woolacombe

North Devon

August 24th 1942

Dear Brian,

Many thanks for your letter last week, and mother thanks you for her birthday letter & wishes. Mother is as Phyllis says "3 score".

As regards our King Edward potatoes they had the "blight" all right, so I got Dadds to lift them & put them in the garage to ripen. I do not suppose I have saved them all – but I afterwards read a Ministry of Agriculture instruction that King Edwards could be lifted on August 15th, about the time ours were done. They seem especially susceptible to the disease. We have only 60 leeks planted, so I can only guess what became of the other 40! Anyhow we have enough as we have quite a lot from seed – now transplanted.

We hope you will enjoy the week's training with the H.G. and not upset the Sergeant Major who wants some "real soldiers". We shall be glad to see you when you can get down. I thought you were entitled to 3 weeks in the year? But I suppose not in war time.

We have had severe winds most of the summer. Runner beans blown off the sticks & leaves torn off, the maize coming up well but blown over by the wind. Everything in the garden being blown about sometimes from one direction & then from another. The air is seldom still long. Phyllis says that at Downderry where she is there is seldom any wind – so they welcome any wind to stir the stagnant air, and this in Cornwall!

My dear Brian

Thank you very much for your letters & good wishes. I had quite a bundle on Saturday, Phyllis & Auntie May's letters this morning. So, I am now 60 years old & not likely to be called up – for a while – it was splendid of you all to remember & lovely to have so many good wishes. Auntie lily came back with me on Saturday from the Restaurant & filthy day again & coming home I was splashed all over the rain having all mud again. It soon dries up however & yesterday & today quite summer like.

Do you remember the Browns at Mr. Woggetts Christmas Party. Mr. B has an artificial leg, his sister has come to Woolacombe with a friend & staying at Castle Rock, so I asked them to tea yesterday & heard all the news of Chenies Ave. (*previous home in Chalfont, built by William.)* Auntie Lily made a jam sandwich (*cake*) with 3 of our own eggs & it was a treat & very much appreciated by the visitors, she excels in that kind of cake.

One hen went broody again, the young one & I shut her up for several days & let her out this morning. Charles sent me 3 china eggs & the same day I put them in the nests ----- *(Seperated sheet probably comes next)*

3. ---------old hen lays beside it, funny isn't it? Auntie asked Dorothy to look out for some & so another arrived for me from David's John! Well I shall be able to train the pullets with them I hope.

Did we tell you that we cooked one cockerel for Sunday when Ronald & Charles came, the meat was a horrid piece, so I got the Farmer's wife to kill it & I did the rest, but I got their lice on me which is horrible. Will you ask Mrs. Shepherd what she does about plucking, if it's better to let the bird get cold first.

A lot of the maize is lying down. I wonder if another year it was sown close together more like corn whether one would hold up the other, but I suppose not. I have righted them once or twice, but the winds persist. The garden is doing well really. I have cut 12 cucumbers from the frame, one this morning weighs 17 ounces. There are a fine lot of tomatoes, but they ripen slowly.

Our farmer is having a job with his corn, so blown about, they can only cut one way, it's to be hoped fine weather will last to get it dry & carried.

I do hope you will enjoy the H.G. exercises & find the new survey work more interesting.

I do hope you feel none the worse for the blood transfusion & teeth out, rather much to lose all together surely.

All right, we won't think anything about Miss Jennings, but hope you will tell us when Miss Right comes along.

Ronald & Charles went somewhere each day. Charles said that Ronald must be trying to slim him, they walked so far. Their last day (*they*) took (*a*) bus to Ilfracombe, then bus to Combemartin & walked from there to Hunters Inn where they had tea & back to Combemartin. Charles used to fall asleep on the couch after supper most evenings, the air made him sleepy, his work is mostly in the greenhouses. He wrote a most appreciative letter afterwards, had never been asked to stay anywhere before.

Must get on to some other letters now, so with many thanks & love shall look forward to seeing you later on.

Yours ever affectionately Mother

July 4th to 10th Convoy PQ 17 (Allied Convoy bound for Russia) was attacked by torpedo bombers and dive-bombers. The Admiralty gave the order for the convoy to scatter. The convoy lost a total of 23 merchant ships that carried 430 tanks, 210 planes, 3,350 vehicles and nearly 100,000 tons of cargo.

August 19th The decision was made to evacuate the survivors from an unsuccessful attack on Dieppe.

Down Top
Poole Lane
Woolacombe
N. Devon
Saty, 26/9/42

Dear Brian

Many thanks for your P.C. recd' the other day when you were on the H.G. course. Very glad you were enjoying it. Perhaps you wouldn't have enjoyed it so much if you had the present weather. The weather here during that week was mainly fine but since last Sunday has been very wet, cold & windy, and nothing much could be done in the garden. The farmer here, managed eventually to get his corn harvest in, but it was difficult. As the agricultural reports for the country said a week ago that about ¾ of the corn harvest had been gathered, I imagine that nothing could have been done since then & so I suppose there will be a good deal of loss. Bumper harvests are not much good if the weather prevents them being gathered. Taking the summer as a whole it has been miserable here – with a few fine days now & then. The week you spent here was one of the best.

Mother has got rid of her 5 cockerels and now has 2 hens & 6 pullets are all together. The hens have stopped laying and the pullets haven't started, so we are in a bad way just now for eggs. However, the fowls are eating alright, so we must live in hopes.

As regards your question about bulbs & carnations, mother says she hasn't any ground prepared for them and doesn't think she can do with them – thank you very much. Dadds hasn't been coming lately, partly owing to the weather & partly owing to another man being away at the School where he works.

Mother would like, however, an Echinops – if you are able to obtain one – our gardening book says that the best of the genus is Echinops Retro. * Do not worry about it if it is difficult to obtain.

Uncle Ernest, Kathleen & her baby were at Woolacombe recently for a fortnight, and had some of the best weather of the Summer. We saw them about 4 times. They seemed to have enjoyed their holiday.

I hope you are feeling more settled in your job & keeping well. We are about the same as usual.

With love

Your affec father WJL

* *Inserted here from Alice*

& a young Bay tree? Miss Wallers lanky one eventually died. What with needlework, knitting & house I have done no gardening at all this year beyond looking after the frame & tomatoes & ----- *squashed in at the top of letter* ----everywhere is smothered in weeds. Has the baby arrived yet; hope Mrs.Shepherd is keeping well & that all will be well with her. Am making some garments for Phyllis Walker's children (*Phyllis Walker's husband had been to school with Ronald in London*) as well as Twitcher's Nursery.

September 25th The Germans attack Stalingrad but were halted by the Russians. They attacked again on 4th October and fierce fighting followed for 3 weeks.

1943

Down Top
Poole Lane
Woolacombe
N. Devon
Jany 12th 1943

Dear Brian,

Thanks for your letter of the 1st. Glad you got back in reasonable time. It was nice to have you & Ronald here again – a pity Phyllis couldn't get home. She talks of asking for leave – soon – and spending part of it with Vera Grant of Worcester, on her way home.

The fowls are still delivering the goods. Sometimes as many as 30 per week. I hope Mr. Shepherd's are also doing their duty.

We heard from Ronald recently, that you & he met in Maidstone by accident – that you had put up at the best Hotel in town. Hope you enjoyed the pruning course – but it must have been an expensive week for you. However, as a bachelor, I suppose doesn't matter very much.

We hope you do get Shepherd's job, that is if you want it, and if you have to move to Lyndhurst – it will only be moving a bit earlier, after all.

My dear Brian,

Thank you for your nice letter & glad you were able to go to Maidstone after all, it made a nice change. Mr. Dadds has not been here for several weeks, so very glad you did our pruning for us. We have had some samples of weather recently, hail, snow for a day, & gales of wind with rain, the garden is a swamp almost. I am glad Mr. Norman strengthened the fowl house or I should have had no peace of mind some nights.

As Daddy told you the pullets have got into their stride & are laying at least 4 a day, sometimes more.

Auntie Lily has been to stay at Parkham for 2 days last week. Harry was home on leave, she was here last weekend & seems pretty well, but has booked a room in a Guest House in Ilfracombe in a suitable position & Harry is going to increase her allowance to enable her to live there. The room will be vacant in 3 weeks time. I wrote to Dorothy telling her of her Mother's condition & she phoned later to say that after the boys return to school, she will come down to help in the clearing up. Harry & Dorothy will have what they want & the rest will be sold. It's rather a wrench after all but Auntie is taking it very well.

I heard from Mrs. Russell that Peggy is living at home in a flat upstairs with her baby daughter just over 1 month, her husband is in the middle East & Alan transferred to the Indian Army & was on his way there.

I started to weed the border behind the fowl run, then it rained & I had to stop there have been few days without rain or the wind is too wild.

We shall be glad to hear how you get on re- the new job if you get it & new digs. I have finished the Berlin Diary & found it most interesting if you want it passed on to anyone else, let me know.

Love Mother

10th January The VI Army of German troops in Stalingrad were attacked by the Russians. They were defeated and marched to prison camps.

Letter from Ronald Lowries

21 College Rd

Maidstone

23rd II 1943

Dear Brian,

Very many thanks for your letter of 21st Jan & for sending on the book. I enjoyed reading it & have now returned it to mother. I think it is one of the most human books I have read for a long time. Poor little Father Chisholm *, he seemed to catch it in the neck wherever he was! Yet his sincerity shows up far above all the other characters in the story.

As you see from the above, I have changed my residence. It is a slight improvement but nothing to shout about. I have a larger room & a wardrobe & a cupboard & am on the ground floor instead of the attic. The old dear is rather parsimonious about firing & lighting etc. The lamp in the room where I am now writing was a 25 watt & had an opal shade below it. I found my eyes giving me trouble so suggested that the light was hardly adequate. She replied that all her other gentlemen (since departed elsewhere of course) had managed perfectly happily. So now I substitute a 60 watt lamp of my own when I am writing, much to her chagrin. Still I am paying extra for the juice it consumes.

Her ideas are rather comic. She cuts sausages down the middle lengthways & gives you three halves. I suppose she thinks you have been led to believe that you have three whole ones.

Oh well, one must not grumble, it could be a whole lot worse & would be in the Army, which reminds me that I had my medical yesterday week & was passed Grade I. Whether or not I shall be called up they will have to fight out between themselves.I really don't mind which happens now that I have had to shift from Worthing, although I would rather keep my hand in on my own line.

I wonder whether you have shifted jobs and/or digs? I hope you will find a comfortable place when you do have to move.

I am sending some letters which Daddy sent me a few days ago & which will give you the latest information about Bob & Phyllis.

How is H.G. going? I have got into the Intelligence Pltn (*platoon*) of H.G. coy (*company)*. It is rather interesting work with plenty of map reading etc. We have a very enthusiastic I (*instructor?*) officer who takes us for 5 or so miles on Sunday mornings, tramping around this area, learning the district & taking stock of distances, cover etc.

While I think of it, my friend Charles would be grateful for any spare literature on recent research etc in Horti (*Horticulture*) which might come your way. He takes the "Gardener" (*magazine*) I believe, but is not in the way of getting much "pukka gen". I am hoping that when I have a decent place where he could stay, that he will spend a weekend here. Do you think there would be any possibility of visiting the **E. Malling Research Station?

Well I must close. I hope you are keeping fit.

All the best.

Your affec bro, Ronald

**Father Francis Chisholm was the main character in the book The Keys of the Kingdom written in 1941 by A. J. Cronin. It was later made into a film in 1944.*

***East Malling Research Station in Kent was established in 1913, and specialized in horticultural and agricultural research, especially fruit production.*

Down Top

Poole Lane

Woolacombe

N. Devon

March 18th 43

Dear Brian,

We received the seeds you so kindly ordered for us, a short while ago, and mother has been busy sewing (sic) them, many thanks.

We heard from Ronald recently, telling us about Colin Waldrain's wedding which he attended at Edgware. He says he quite enjoyed it. Wedding in Church at Edgware and reception at the girl's parents at Hampstead. Ronald said that he had sent you some letters from Bobby and Phyllis which I sent him. I have just sent Ronald four more letters – perhaps they will reach you in turn. Bobby had left Ireland. He wrote to us from Woolwich but doesn't say if he is going back to Ireland. Perhaps he doesn't know. Phyllis came home on leave early in the month for 7 days – and had fine weather and appears to have enjoyed herself in her quiet way. She is back in Ireland at a new station. Has obtained a further stripe, and is now a "Section officer" equal to Lieut in the army. Her address is: -

s/o P. W. Lowries W.A.A.F.

R.A.F. Ballymartin

Home Forces

The weather has been lovely lately, but our garden is looking awful – weeds everywhere- old Dadds – who is here today – only comes now and then. Once in 2 or 3 weeks – but if we complained he might not come at all. We are not growing so many potatoes this year, a few "Sharp's Express" and a few "King Edward". We can always buy potatoes and want more ground for green stuff.

Hope you are keeping well

Your affect father

WJL

Bobby's memoir says that he had been ill in Ireland, and had spent three weeks in hospital in Belfast, with gastro-enteritis. He had previously described the poor sanitary conditions in his barracks. Phyllis visited him in hospital there, as she was stationed in Ireland at the time. He was discharged from a convalescent camp on 8th March, 1943, and was sent back to England.

The following is an extract from Bobby's memoir.

"I arrived back at Woolwich at 6pm on the 9th March and reported in. Before the war, the Depot was enclosed by high railings, but these had been removed and melted down to help the war effort. Consequently, although you entered by the main gate (which had also gone) anybody could come and go whenever they wished to do so! There were also individuals like myself, being posted in and out all the time, so it would be difficult to keep an accurate check. Some of the men who lived in London would slip off home after

any parades they were supposed to be on had taken place. ....Occasionally, they would check the barrack rooms at midnight, and found there were empty beds and kit which did not tally with any records, and it was believed they were men who had been "absent without leave" and had "run out" of money, even though they had been living in the camp, and sometimes receiving pay!

Bob managed to get a weekend pass, and went to visit his wife, Joan, in Ealing. A week later, he was posted to the 9th Reserve AA Battery at Husbands Bosworth in Leicestershire. A week after this, he was granted 10 days leave, during which time he was visited by Brian. Perhaps, this information was passed around the family in the letters they exchanged, but possibly not because of the Censor. Bob had kept a diary and years later was able to recount his experiences in detail.

Down Top

Poole Lane

Woolacombe

N. Devon

June 29th 1943

Dear Brian,

Thanks for your letter of the 21st Inst. Glad you are still at the old address & comfortable.

It must have been a very strenuous weekend with the H.G. The weather was good though. The weather here just now is very warm & sunny, like your holiday weather last year!

Your onions are looking a little better but not much – the soil is unsuitable for onions I think. The carrots look very poor and we do not expect any results. We are going to ask Dadds to sew (sic) some more. The potatoes have the blight earlies & main crop, not very badly – owing we think to a lot of mists. I went over each plant & removed the diseased leaves & burnt them. They are looking much better in the sunshine.

The chickens are alright. We haven't done anything more with the wire etc. I suppose one day, when we want to separate the cockerels we shall do something about it.

Phyllis has written to say that she is bringing Vera to stay here from July 25th (Sunday) to July 31st (Saturday) As she will not be here for a week end, it is no use suggesting that you come home to see her. She wants to spend the remainder of her leave with Vera at a Cottage near Worcester.

Bobby wrote recently that Elaine's husband "Tim" passed away on June 9th. He had pneumonia & then an abscess on the brain. Poor chap!

Glad you are keeping well

With love

Your affec father WJL

Daddy seems stumped for news, well there isn't any really, only odds & ends. I think of something especially to tell you when working about, it seems important at the time!

The tomatoes are coming along well. I gave them some fertilizer from last year's tin just after you went back & thought of using that first.

If you could write down for me how much to use of the various fertilizers we bought & what each is best for which & whether to use dry & how often, it would be a great help for I forget so easily.

Sulphate of ammonia I know, but the Muriate of Chalk or Potash am very uncertain about.

I blew Derris dust on the carrots last night but they are disappearing. Dadds said they hadn't the fly, but something is eating them. Mrs. Lucas came up one day for some sprout plants & was interested in your trial lettuces.

I rang up Trumps today to order some mixed wallflower & Sweet William seed, these have been such a success & Pyrethrum Pwd (*powder*) but they have none, nor has Swift; but Trumps will send Nicotine Pwd. Mrs. Lucas says that is best for carrots, is that right.

Brian and Mr. and Mrs. Lucas relaxing in front of beach huts on Woolacombe sands, later in 1948

Written squashed at the top of the letter upside down was added - The new gate & wiring is a great success & help to me & I wonder how I managed for so long with the other bits & pieces. Thank you for everything.

April 19th Start of the Warsaw Uprising.

May 17th The German army in North Africa surrendered to the British and Americans.

Down Top

Poole Lane

Woolacombe

N.Devon

July 12 – 43

My dear Brian,

Very many thanks for your letter rec[d] this morning & all the information it will be most useful to keep by us for I must confess that my brain gets quite addled with so many different insecticides & fetilizers.

Thank you very much for the food masher & rings for the fowls, the latter I have not used yet, but shall do so very soon.

The chopper instrument I find splendid, it really cuts the food splendidly (repeating myself) sign of old age. Anyhow I am most grateful for it & the rings & shall regard them as my birthday present.

I am also grateful for the new gate & wire enclosure, it is a great help to be able to go in & out so easily, especially in bad weather. It turned all day on Saturday, heavy cold rain whilst waiting for the bus in the morning & when I returned at 3.30 it was dripping from me, then a gale sprang up & lasted all Sunday with thick fog & rain, the fowl run last night was almost a pond & poor chicks looked a sorry sight; their coops a mass of wet stuff, but I couldn't do anything about it until today & have thoroughly cleaned them out & set them up to dry.

The young hen has started to lay, she is still with her chicks but expect I shall soon move her, I was waiting to let the chicks grow a bit more & so be able to stand up to the big ones.

The farmer says that his potatoes up on Brackenridge have got the blight badly & when the sun comes out he expects that will stink for miles, he has promised me a bag of chats when he digs them, for I am stumped now, no old ones to be had, & nothing any good from next door. Mr. S. says that he is not touching the old ones if he can help it for the Barum man bought a ton & he's just got a mess of rotted stuff on his hands & they can't buy less than a ton, they are released too late to be of any use.

I think next door are feeding the farm dog, & old potatoes they had over, they fed to some calves over the fence, so! they can go without eggs, but they annoy me by putting over a lot of turnip tops & radish tops. Daddy told them once that I had to take it to the compost heap, trust him to do the plain speaking. They have a field of waving weeds also & high up above our fence near the clothes post a mass of nettles. I suppose the farmer hasn't time to cut it for them & they don't bother, the boys may burn it down when they come home, but that's in a fortnights time.

The tomatoes are getting badly spotted leaves. I have taken some of the worst off & will fumigate when the weather is suitable again, will that stop it? We can't find anything about (it) in our books.

Your trial lettuces are looking well but it's the lime only that are the largest & must be flourishing so far. I have had some nice hearty ones from the original rows, got some today, nearly the last of those. Your onions are growing now & looking bigger & better, you don't have to peer at them to see them now & of the onion sets, some of those are getting very big.

I gathered a handful of peas yesterday, they are not quite ready yet; but some broad beans were quite good, our first of either. The spinach is doing well & we have had 2 pickings. Raspberries are very fine, but the lanes are too thick & so some are not good & it's a job to get between, but I have bottled some & given some & no doubt can pick again tonight.

The strawberries are very sweet from your plants, one or two plants look like pegging out; but they get full sun & so the berries benefit; raspberries are not sweet this year.

I have collected pounds of slugs huge black & brown, they come out of the borders in the evening & I go round with a pail of salt water & I have had hundreds, but the farmer on Sunday morning said he saw literally thousands on the grass next door, so where will they go & what happens to them. I find the fowls won't eat them, the chicks like the tiny ones only.

I have made two nice little blouses for small boys out of your grey & blue short sleeved shirts. Matron came up on Sat week & took away some things, but they still want more she has 15 big ones (4 ish) she wants to set up but of course they each want several changes & then if they go home, she has to let them have some clothes – their own are not very good.

The sun is shining again, so that's an improvement but the wind is still rough & plants are knocked down & broken.

The sea holly you got for me is a different variety from the one I had, bluer foliage & finer type, so am glad, the other has very coarse foliage. I saw the one I had in mind in a shop in Ilfracombe & asked its name & they said it was a Scotch Thistle – it is very blue with a collar all round like the Winter Aconite.

I wanted to tell you that many of the tomato flower stems have split into 3 or 4 slender ones. I expect they ought to be cut off. Is it for want of fertilizer? they are too slender to bear any weight & most of the plants are doing this near the top.

Well you will say it's all about the garden.

I hope the Kellers enjoy their holiday, they must have had a horrid time yesterday but no doubt the weather is on the mend, we shall be pleased to see them if they come this way.

Harry Watkins has gone to N. Africa, was given 48 hours to prepare. Things seem to be moving there now again.

With much love & hope you have been able to settle down comfortably.

Yours ever affectionately

Mother

The following is the second half of a letter from around the same time, possibly slightly earlier than the one above.

2. ---- Both she & Daddy were putting their money on those without fertilizer! But that's the way of this ground, they come & look promising & just stagnate!

The cucumbers are just getting along, not much growth yet; but we have had a few nice little strawberries & the raspberries are coming in now, very fine some of them. I confess to having kept the strawberry basket & used it this morning to pick well over a pound – I should think only 2nd picking. When Daddy goes to post he will take them to Mrs. Norman, they are very good to us in so many ways.

I have taken old hen from the big chicks & put her with her daughters & very soon she was having a fight with a brown pullet. I've never seen it before, a silent tussle at combs & wattles, hanging on to each other, it lasted quite a while & old hen looked very messy – comb bleeding in several places. She started laying again but I think I will get Mr. Hopkins to do her for Phyllis & Vera's visit. The white & black cockerels have started trying to crow, it's a very queer noise. I've been slug hunting at night & get a filthy lot in a pail of salt water!

The big grey foliaged bush with yellow flowers is now a picture & hangs over the verge.

Phyllis sent me a very nice white silk blouse yesterday from Belfast: I badly needed a new one & by the way, Daddy had his suit fitted last Wednesday, we wonder when he will get it. Your people sound very nice & I hope you will be happy & comfortable with them.

Please tell Mrs. Keller that we shall be pleased to see them if they can get here from Lynton. We could perhaps put them up for a night or is it rash to offer to do so, I leave it to you. I hope the christening went off happily & that you will like your God son & that Ian has quickly recovered from the measles. With much love

Mother

July 10th Britain and America invaded Sicily.

Down Top

Poole Lane

Woolacombe

N. Devon

August 9th 1943

Dear Brian

Thankyou for your letter of 21st July and the news etc.

This is to wish you many happy returns of 11th and as they say in the East - "may your shadow never grow less". We hope you are settling down in your new home. The house, of course, is new even if the address is the same. I wonder if you have been able to get the use of the same garage for your car again.

You say that the ground is thoroughly soaked through. That is so here, for about a week, including the weekend it has rained more or less continuously and everything is very moist & bedraggled – also strong winds – much of the maize has been damaged – about 12 plants simply broken off. We have had a few peas – no runners yet, but plenty of blossom.

Phyllis & Vera had a good week here - not much rain & several hot days. They travelled here from Worcester by night & back again by night. "It makes the holiday seem longer" so they say but travelling conditions were awful. Phyllis appreciated your phone call – after spending a week in a cottage near Worcester, Phyllis, we think is crossing to Ireland today. She flew from Belfast to Liverpool when coming here, which cost her £3 whereas if she had come by boat it wouldn't have cost her anything. She wanted the experience and also to cut out nearly a day.

Hope you had a good time with the Shepherds at the Bank holiday weekend. The weather here was none too good.

Ronald hasn't fixed up any date to come down here. He said he thought of coming during August. Lilian is coming here on the 21st for a week. She wanted a fortnight's holiday and her mother can only arrange for a week in Ilfracombe.

As regards leeks – I really think we have enough thank you.

Well don't get too hilarious on Wednesday. (*Brian's birthday*)

With love

Your affect father WJL

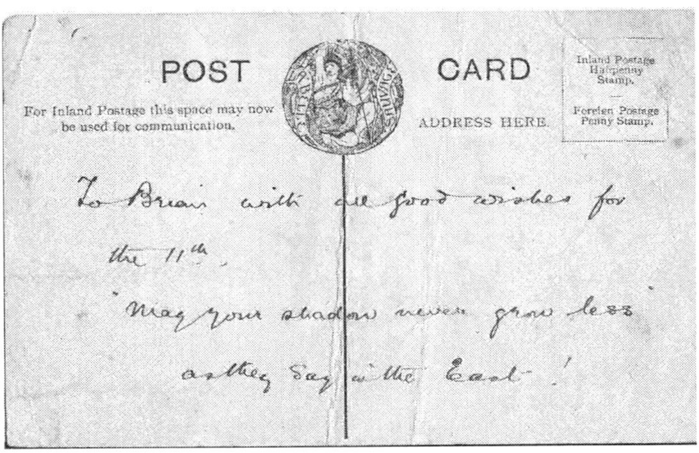

Postcard from WJL, undated, but with the same quotation as in the letter.

The reverse of the postcard.

(Brian and his father both enjoyed reading Dickens.)

My dear Brian

Just a few lines to add my love & best wishes for your birthday. We have no coupons between us or I would have bought you some colored handkys (sic), which you seem to need, so please accept the enclosed stamps, they are always useful & necessary.

The tomatoes are coming along with huge trusses, but we need more sunshine to ripen. The farmers also want it for the corn, it's lying down & looking awful since the heavy rain & wind & one time it looked like a carpet, so smooth. However, it was much the same last year & Mr. Hopkins had a bumper crop. The lime sample of lettuces are still the best, they need thinning out; so thick, but I have been using from the old rows first.

Phyllis & Vera had a good feed of peas & enjoyed their meals, especially Vera with plenty of milk & eggs. Phyllis does not go short of those things over there. Cucumbers are forming at last & one is several inches long.

The strawberry plants look very well & sending out plenty of runners, one or two plants died, the few strawberries were very sweet.

I can't see any Dianthus seedlings coming. Mrs. Lucas brought me a fine lot of Anemone corms, they were given her & she shared with me, so I hope they will do well.

The new carrots are not doing well either, I put some broken carbon over the ground, thinking to take the place of napthalene.

The hens are slowly giving up laying, several have been broody in turn. I have put the big pullet chicks with the hens & the cockerels in the small division with a piece of netting to act as a gate.

The 2nd brood are still uncertain whether they will be cocks or hens so they have the middle run to themselves. It is a great boon having it so nicely divided, thanks to you.

You didn't say how the christening went off, hope you enjoyed the party & that the Shepherds have settled down in their new house & like it there, expect you noticed a difference in the baby, not having seen her for some time.

Poor Auntie Elsie is in a very bad way, can't speak at all now & very depressed, no wonder, poor thing. Her sister writes to me about her. She has been in Farmboro' Hospital & I told Dorothy, who went to see her last week but they won't keep her there because she is not physically ill & they want the bed. The husband & sisters don't know what to do with her, they can't get any help, it is most pathetic.

Uncle Herbert writes that he has had an offer for some plot of land opposite the bungalow. I think Daddy will accept it.

The news is better isn't it; I hope the Germans can't hold out much longer.

With much love, hoping you are very well.

Yours ever affectionately

Mother

Written at the top of the letter as an after thought.

Mrs. Curtis wrote me concerning Joan, could I find her some light employment – near me & somewhere to lodge, not too far from me, says she is fond of gardening !!!

I wrote saying this was an out – of – the –way quiet hole etc etc. No doubt wanted me to have her here & take her off their hands, she said they only got on her nerves. We might turn this into a mental home.

July 25th Mussolini was arrested

July 28th A bombing raid on Hamburg resulted in a firestorm that killed more than 50,000 people.

August 6th German troops entered Italy which prevented any chance of a peace settlement taking Italy out of the war.

Undated. Probably Summer 1943

My dear Brian,

I have just had to write a letter of condolence & they are so difficult to write. Do you remember Mr. Smart who sold plants at school at the big 3 day Sale, he died a few years ago, now his young daughter Joan died on Monday. Mrs. Smart is a Yorkshire woman, living in Finchley,she used to bake all this bread, brown & white & made marvellous cakes for the Sale. I liked her very much.

I have been hearing from Mrs. Hill lately she has just taken on the Vice Pres: of the Parents Guild & wrote asking me for patterns etc, so I almost feel as tho' I belong again, hearing about old members, there is no mentions of Mrs Bill Hughes, so I presume she has dropped out.

We are wondering what has happened or will happen in the re-shuffle process & very interested to hear all about it & the results. I hope you get something really definite. You must have had a very busy time with your shows & judging & so glad to hear of the success at the Horse Show.

Your gas exercises are very thorough & it helps one to remember so much better with practical demonstrations.

We require a refresher course by now. I have promised Mrs. Hill, near here to go with her to Home Nursing Classes which may start quite soon at Mortehoe, it means a long walk once a week, but not so far as to the Castle Rock Hotel, where the gas Lectures were held.

Down below is a very busy place these days & promises to drive out the inhabitants, but that remains to be seen, there are plenty of rumours.

I managed to release Pushkin one Sunday morning from a trap in Brackenridge, he sat up patiently whilst I struggled to open the thing, he must have been there, probably all night. Just at first he is very quiet but as the numbness wears off, he cries a lot & tells us all about it, what his legs will be like in time doesn't bear thinking about, the trappers will be coming round here soon. I have been trying to think out dinner for an invasion of four tomorrow. They cannot expect a lavish table these days, the best of it is, that Winnie writes vaguely about coming & how many there will be. She is getting married next year she says to a farmer's son.

I went down with Auntie Lily to the P.O. one day. Auntie had had lunch here to break the journey & then we walked. Uncle Sidney seemed quite friendly but not Auntie Lucy. She didn't even ask Auntie Lily to sit down, we went on to Mrs. Connibears who had asked us to tea. (*Sidney and Lucy Ridd kept the Post Office at Mortehoe until November 1943)*

There was the question of Dorothy & China which they were minding & wanted to get rid of, so I offered to have it. They gave it to the grocer to bring up on Monday. I am glad they are going & shall feel freer to go down there than before. Strange how the Ridds are getting nearer together. Harry lives near Barnstaple, Fred not far away & Bessie also & now Sid is joining the group.

My pullets are laying very tiny eggs, but the hens are seriously moulting & looking scraggy & are resting from their labours.

I have had about an hour trying to weed this week, there are masses of everything wild & then I feel I ought to be sewing, they need such a lot of knickers they say at the Nursery & I have plenty of material, so feel that should come first.

It's wonderful news about Joan's successfull (sic) year with over £500 in the bank not now of course since re-paying the £100 to us.

Well now I must add a postscript to Bobby's letter, so will dry up.

With love from us both, trust you are keeping well

Yours ever affectionately   Mother

Down Top

Poole Lane

Woolacombe

N.Devon

Sept 3rd 1943

Dear Brian,

Many thanks for your letter of Aug 14th. Also mothers' on her birthday.

The weather here is still dismal. It rains every day & most nights. The local farmers have had a most anxious time getting in the harvest which will be very light. Devon seems to be a very wet county, at any rate this year. I haven't had to do any watering. Lillian came for a fortnight, and this is her second week. She seems to have enjoyed herself – but no basking in the sun!

Glad you had a nice weekend with the Shepherds. As regards Mrs. S's sister I thought the airman wasn't "her cup of tea", perhaps you were, and escaped "as usual". However, there is yet time –

As regards Ronald & his courting, the lady is not the one who came to Chalfont for a weekend. She was, however, one of the party on the Cruise with Ronald & Phyllis. Another thought she was very nice. Unfortunately, during the London Blitz, she contracted "shelter Tuberculosis", and was under treatment for a long time. The Dr. says she is now quite free of the complaint, but naturally Ronald is somewhat nervous.

Ronald intends coming home for a week on Sept 18th, but not with Stephanie as she has already refused several visits to friends owing to the strain of traveling during these times.

As regards Phyllis' flying. It was rather a "flop", as owing to obscured glass in the plane she couldn't see anything only experienced being "bumped about" in the air. It saved time however. She left Belfast in the afternoon & arrived in Liverpool at 6pm. We haven't heard from her since she arrived back in Ireland, nearly 4 weeks and rather wonder why.

Bobby was transferred to the R.A.V.C. in July and is hoping to join the "War Dogs" soon. Joan sent a large hamper of apples – chiefly cookers – We are very glad as the apples in this District were a failure and old Harris cannot supply us this year as he did last.

I suppose Lord Wolver's Estate will be selling Cox's presently. I am watching the adverts for their notice.

Hope you will have a good time in Leeds if you go on the 15th.

With love

Yours affect father

WJL

P.S.

I started this letter on 1st and mother was going to add to it, thanking you for your wishes & phone. However, she hasn't had a minute to do any writing and hasn't been in the greenhouse for a week.

Lillian has been here for a fortnight on Saturday & what with house work – fowls, mending for "Twitchers" etc she finds herself with no leisure to sit down to write.

I know you will understand. She thanks you very much for the poultry rings & food chopper, which saves her a lot of time

Hope you are well WJL

September 3rd Britain and America invaded Italy.

Down Top

Poole Lane

Woolacombe

N.Devon

September 14- 43

My dear Brian,

Yesterday, a box of plants arrived from John Forbes, Hawick, Scotland. I am sure you must have ordered them & thank you very much for them. Just the things I like & do well here, Violas, Phlox, Pyrethrums, & the little blue thistle which I can't spell or pronounce. You shouldn't give me so much you know. I planted them in a piece of cleared ground opposite the fowls last night, & hope to find them a more suitable home when I've weeded the other beds.

The weather is still atrocious, we had a thunder storm on Sunday & torrents of rain almost ever since, for the past week we have had heavy rain every night & the ground is saturated.

We had a card from Ronald this morning to say that he & Charles will be coming on Saturday, but that he must return the following Friday for the Maidstone Birthday (Crusader) on Saturday. I hope the weather improves before they come. We have had a river all round the front of the house all the morning, but it is drying up a bit now.

Mr. Swift collected my six smaller cockerels & gave me 32/- (*shillings*) for them, he said they had fine big frames, but wanted filling out! I'm glad to be rid of them, the feeding was becoming a problem.

Now, Matron at the Nursery is saving potato peelings for me. I have had 2 enormous lots from there, 2 of the girls push them along in a pram.

In order to get more meal I have 4 people's shell egg ration, the Hills, Miss Roberts, & Aunties so that will make the feeding easier. The last few weeks the hens were laying quite well but 2 are broody again, & all are moulting more or less, but I have pickled ones to fall back on & my customers have had so few eggs that they will be very content with one or two a week each.

Auntie Lily has a Miss Ponton staying with her for a fortnight, Mrs. Ponton & her daughter lived in the flat below Auntie at Bromley, she has stayed with Auntie before at Apsby Terrace.

There was no bedroom available for Lillian where Auntie lives, so she stayed the 2 weeks here & went into Ilfracombe most days. We all three had lunch one day at Auntie's expence at Southcombes & went afterwards to see the film "Gone with the Wind". Have you seen it? A four hour show, but keeps it's interest in a remarkable way.

How interesting for you to meet Mr. Joseph (*Mcleod – added later*) at the Eastleigh Show, have you many such events on your list of appointments? I expect you are in Leeds now & I hope you have an enjoyable week there & meet people you know.

We shall hope that you will be able to come down for Christmas. I am trying to keep speckled bird for that occasion instead of ordering an expensive turkey. He has grown a wonderful looking specimen with beautiful plumage. I have resigned from the B.R. the rush is over & I hope that Auntie will do the same in a short while, she will be 75 on the 22nd & has not been too well lately, but as Lillian said, she always wants to go one better than anyone else.

We went gleaning one evening with Miss Brown & whereas Lillian, Miss B & I carried 2 sheaves, Auntie must carry 3 & uphill too, a thing I avoid with her always. The farmer has had awful weather for his corn, one newly ploughed field sheaves were lying around under the hedge, cut by hand.

Dr Brian,

As Miss Roberts has just called & prevented mother finishing her letter I am finishing it for her. Hope you are well & enjoying better weather than we are. It has been a most dismal & disappointing summer.

Love from us both

Your affec father

WJL.

Down Top

Poole Lane

Woolacombe

N.Devon

Oct 13th 1943

Dear Brian,

Many thanks for your long letter of 26th Sept with all your news.

Ronald & his friend Charles were here for a week, and had very fair weather including one or two really fine days. They tried one day to get to Clovelly, but like Phyllis & her friend Vera didn't get further than Bideford. One day they altered part of the fowl run so that the fowls can go into the farmer's field, for a change from their run. They (the fowls) do not go into the field very much but are soon back on their run.

Phyllis is still in Ireland and we wrote to her for her birthday on the 3rd. She replied saying that she was well but very busy and not writing to anyone for sometimes long spells. She did not write for mother's birthday, as when she noticed the date it was already too late to write in time and the same thing happened at your birthday. She not only has to supervise the technical work, but the admin side also, and has little leisure. She expects to get a few days leave at the end of this month or November – but not at Xmas.

It will be very nice if you can take the remainder of your holiday at Xmas. I do not think we want any more alterations to the fowl run, but mother is always full of ideas!!

As regards the garden – we have had a nice lot of marrows – the runners have been fair – not prolific. There was no trench previously prepared for them. The trench prepared for runners was used for marrows as we changed the site of the marrows. The tomatoes have been a fair crop – about 50lbs instead of 70 or 80 lbs last year. All the plants suffered from the fungus disease, and towards the end, most of the leaves were removed. It didn't affect the fruit however, which were as nice as usual.

Charles brought some tomatoes, and a huge basket of grapes, which we quite enjoyed, also some Cox's apples. He has since sent some huge pears & small eating apples. The tomatoes Charles brought were called "Veto – mold", not subject to the fungus, but they tasted very sweet, more like fruit than tomatoes and mother didn't care for them very much.

Bobby has been transferred to the "War Dogs Training School" at Potters Bar. I return his letter to you with the present address in case you want it. Bobby says they have had a very successful year with the Kennels. He has returned the £100 he borrowed from me when they were in difficulties soon after they started. Joan must have worked very hard – she is having a fortnight's holiday this month near Bobby at Potters bar.

We were very interested in the news of your activities professionally and with the H.G., especially about the various gases & chemical smoke etc. You will not be sorry no doubt when something definite is settled at the office.

Uncle Sidney & Aunt Lucy are returning from the P.O. which they sold to a Birmingham man. They are going to live in a house at Pilton near Barnstaple.

Winnie Vellacott is having a holiday this week in Barnstaple, and we expect her to dinner tomorrow with perhaps Harry Ridd & his wife – so it will be a busy day for mother; who has had a cold which is now better.

Hope you are well

With love from us both

Your affec father

WJL

Down Top

Poole Lane

Woolacombe

N.Devon

Nov 1st 1943

Dear Brian,

Many thanks for your letter & good wishes on my birthday – also for mother's letter enclosed.

I hope the office reshuffle results in some benefit to you either in position or salary, or both.

Ronald appears to have recovered from his illness and was moving to a new address in Maidstone. Probably he sent you a card giving his new address. Hope the wedding went off all right on Saturday and you managed your part without undue nervousness. The weather has been very fine for 2 or 3 days but yesterday & today wet again.

Phyllis has been moved from Ireland and is just settling in at her new station:-

R.A.F. North Foreland

Broadstairs Kent

She hopes to get some leave soon.

Dorothy is here (Ilfracombe I mean) for a week & leaves on Wednesday or Thursday. They have had rather a rough time at Keston lately after a long period of quietness.

Uncle Sidney & Aunt Lucy moved from the P.O. this weekend. They didn't call here to say goodbye.

Old Dadds has been coming about once a fortnight recently. Last Thursday (a very fine day) he did a good deal of digging. The time before he cut down the old raspberry canes and removed the surplus canes which we sent to a neighbour of Auntie Lily who wanted some.

The yanks are here now and a good deal of gunfire goes on.

Hope you have managed to get rid of your cold.

With love from us both.

Your affec father WJL

Woolacombe Bay and the surrounding area was used by the American military for practise for D Day, from early July 1943. This was due to the similarity of the coast to the French beaches, particularly those code named Utah and Omaha. Large tracts of land were required from local farmers, and the United States Army had demanded that all villagers in the area must be evacuated. However, the British Government refused this request.

At the north end of Woolacombe Beach was the demolition training area, with the billeting area of tents stretching up towards Mortehoe Junction. Morte Point was used as a target by anti-tank guns and seaborne artillery, and as a demonstration area of air-to-ground support firepower. Full-scale amphibious assaults were held on Woolacombe Beach.

Down Top

Poole Lane

Woolacombe

N.Devon

Monday Nov 8th 1943

Dear Brian,

Many thanks for the box of Cox's which arrived safely. You must let me pay for them as we are very glad to have them and I shall remind you of it when we next meet. They are very fine I think.

It was good of Mr. Allardice to lend you the box, which we are returning - also some wrappers which came around the apples I bought from Lord Wolmer's Estate last year. They may be useful sometime.

The weather is still <u>wet</u> but is now also cold. What a Summer & Autumn!!

Hope you are well and things at the office more settled. I wrote to you last week.

With our love

Your affec father

WJL

"Down Top"

Monday 29 -11-43

Dear Brian

Thanks for your letter of the 12th inst.

I hear from Ronald that you were having an interview at Gloucester, and was rather surprised until I rec'd your letter.

Things seem to have been rather shaken up at the office and I hope they have now settled down, and that you have a job to your liking and some increase of pay.

The Americans down here are just getting into their stride – on Friday they had a "field day". Yanks of all kinds all over the place. Two huge ones came down our lane & simply widened the lower part of the lane (below the Simons') by smashing down the hedges on both sides. They are making a terrible mess all over the place, but they say that this is only the beginning. Of course they wanted to have the inhabitants evacuated, but the people protested and the authorities eventually decided not to.

Phyllis is supposed to come home on leave on Friday next for a week, & may bring Vera with her. She <u>recently</u> got your letter sent on her birthday. It was addressed by you to Downderry Home Forces. Downderry was her station in Cornwall. Her last address in Ireland was "Ballymartin Kilkeel Co. Down". It eventually reached her after going to Devon, Bedford, London & Keston & finally Broadstairs.

Ronald is supposed to be coming at Xmas, but I notice that Civil Servants are not to have leave between 23rd & 28th Dec. I don't know if he can come <u>before</u> the 23rd & leave after the 28th.

We are expecting to see you at Xmas and Auntie Lily will be here we expect.

Weather very rough just now.

Love from both

Yours WJL

1944

Down Top
Poole Lane
Woolacombe
N.Devon
Jan 5 – 44

My dear Brian

A very hurried note to enclose with your socks & tie. Afraid the bad pair made (you) feel clumsy & hurt your feet. Let me have any others that need repair also shirts or anything. Auntie & I can do them between us & will be only too pleased.

I am proud to tell you that after setting the trap on Friday night the opposite side of (the) trough, the rat ran right in & was caught with his head right in it. Proud indeed! But! There is still another & I set it last night, but he went to the other side of trough & there was a fairly stiff frost, it's a case of my wits against his, now I know how to set the trap.

Daddy & I are just off to lunch in Ilfracombe so must hurry.

Your ball was much admired at the Nursery & being soft the children are allowed to have it indoors.

Heard from Phyllis & Ronald this morning. Hope you had a good journey back. Ronald was packed in like a sardine & arrived an hour late, got back about 10.00pm & found his landlady away ill, so had to get his own supper.

In haste Much love Mother

January 5th The start of a major Russian offensive into the Ukraine

Down Top
Poole Lane
Woolacombe
N.Devon
January 8th 1944

Dear Brian

Thanks for your letter and the Calendars. They are very nice – one is now in the kitchen and one in the Drawing Room. When we look at them we shall always think of you (or nearly always).

We are glad you enjoyed Xmas at home, but you and Ronald spent a good deal of the time working and we are very grateful for what you did. Old Dadds didn't turn up on Thursday altho it was a fine day.

As regards the spools for the sewing machine – mother says that the heads must be rounded or they will be no use. Thanks for trying. Mother will look out for three nylon tooth brushes when next in Ilfracombe.

Glad the return journey wasn't too bad, and that the "Friday incident" didn't cause any trouble. Ronald arrived home in Maidstone on the Wednesday about 10 pm & found Mrs. Miles away ill and a note for him. So he had to forage for himself. Bad luck!

We hope you will find some decent digs in Lyndhurst district.

Mother is keeping pretty well – We had lunch in Ilfracombe on Wednesday with Auntie Lily who seemed well.

With love from us both

Your affect father WJL

At the top of the letter

We heard from Bobby. They enjoyed the cockerel which was very nice!

Down Top

Poole Lane

Woolacombe

N.Devon

January 21st 1944

Dear Brian

Many thanks for your letter of the 12th inst enclosing two old sewing machine spools & needles. Unfortunately, mother's machine is a Frister & Rossmann and the Singer needles cannot be used in it.

Thanks also for the two batteries for the cycle lamps torch. I have fitted one which is all right, and keeping the other in reserve.

We hope you will soon find suitable diggings in the Lyndhurst district. No doubt you are very wise to avoid the professional landlady if you can. Fancy this being your 9th change of digs. You certainly are not so fortunate as I was. I was still at home with my parents, brother & sister when I was married at 36. Perhaps, however, it may be better for your wife <u>when</u> you do get married. I am afraid I was rather "spoilt" living so long at home – at least so they say.

Hope you had a good time in London last Saturday and enjoyed the "show".

We were unable to get any toothbrushes in Ilfracombe. They are very scarce here.

Phyllis spent a day recently with Dorothy at Keston and stayed the night. Old Dadds hasn't been here since the week before Xmas, but the weather has been simply awful – rain & sea mist etc nearly every day. The sun is out today however.

Your affec father

WJL

Down Top

Poole Lane

Woolacombe

N.Devon

February 7th 1944

Dear Brian,

Many thanks for your recent letter.

We are very glad you have managed to obtain suitable digs. Your experience is quite different to mine as I lived at home until I married at 36, as I think I mentioned before. We hope you have now settled down to the new conditions both at business and in the home.

It is a good thing to have the use of a garage once more, although small.

I can quite understand the difficult staircase in a bungalow – as upstairs rooms are not really intended. However, so long as you always remember to duck your head all will be well.

I had some sad news on Saturday. Mr. Shepherd met with a serious accident (I don't know what kind) and died on Friday morning. If I had still been a Director of the Cameragraph. Coy (*silent movie film system*) they might have expected me to come up & act for a time; but I resigned my Directorship last Summer – in view partly of some such contingency which I feared might happen. It is the suddenness which shocks me.

We heard from Phyllis this morning. She expects to get leave again shortly and may spend a few days here and a few days in London.

The weather is still wild with a sea mist & rain. Saturday was a fine day and for once Mother & I walked to Woolacombe & back up Sandy Lane to get some mangles?

Old Dadds hasn't been here since the week before Xmas – the weather has of course been "foul", but curiously enough several Thursdays (his day) have been fine, if rather windy.

I saw an advt. in "The Daily Telegraph" of Onion Trees* – 3 years old at 12/- a dozen; so I have sent for a dozen from Scotland. The advt. says "Huge crops every year from some plants, hardy, perennial free from onion fly – onions grow in bunches up to 4'0 (*4 ft*) above ground, also another crop grows underground".

I expect you will think I am "easy money". I thought of growing 6 and giving 6 away to neighbours.

We are pretty well, although I had several days in bed last week with a chill on the liver - or so I think it was.

Mother still goes to her Nursing classes and is going this afternoon.

With love from us both

Your affec father WJL

PS Mr. Denny (of Hallswelle Rd) died on December 30th. He was over 80. Went for a walk, took off his overcoat, sat in a chair & then expired!

Mr. Denny had been a neighbour in Golders Green during the First World War. As part of the war effort, both he and William each had an allotment, to grow extra food. "On Sunday mornings, they could be seen walking down the road in their gardening clothes with fork and spade over their shoulders, and William wearing his wooden soled boots". Information from Bobby's memoir.

**Tree onions sometimes called Egyptian onions or walking onions grow very tall and produce a cluster of small onions on the top of the stalk. The heavy weight causes them to bow down to the ground and the small onions to take root and begin another plant – hence the name "walking onions". The plant is theoretically very productive as it can be harvested at its base as well as at the top.*

Brian and his father working in the vegetable garden at DownTop, Mortehoe later in 1948.

Tree onions can be seen growing in the front of the photograph, so William had persevered with them.

Poole Lane

Woolacombe

N.Devon

March 8th 1944

Dear Brian,

Many thanks for your long letter of Feb 29th and all news.

I have not yet heard how Mr.Shepherd met with his accident. It doesn't appear to be known. At the Inquest it was supposed that he slipped whilst boarding a bus in Holborn.

We are glad you are getting settled with the office work and do not dislike the new work notwithstanding the many forms to be filled in.

I quite agree that Woodland Cottage is not a very nice one, and have wondered many times why Grandma bought it.

It is a nuisance that your re-conditioned engine is not quite satisfactory. Hope you will be able to get it remedied.

We are very glad that you find your diggs comfortable. Living in a house where the husband & wife are not too affectionate and do not get on very well has definite drawbacks to my mind. There is always a danger for a single man in this position, and perhaps a change of diggings would be well, if it can be managed.

As regards the onion trees. They are not now 4.0' high but are supposed to grow that height. They are described as being an "improved large variety" of excellent flavour and immune from the onion fly.

Phyllis returned from leave recently. She had about 5 days in London with her friend Vera seeing shows etc., staged in Bloomsbury and only had one noisy night. Then she came on here for 3 or 4 days. Went back with a cold. Mother & I also have colds on the head. The keen N.E. winds I suppose.

Phyllis blamed the cold weather here, but I wonder if she picked it up in London, for we both now have the same kind of heavy cold, such a nuisance, makes one feel disinclined to do much. We are now having a dry spell with sunny days, but I've not yet had time to do anything in the garden, too much to do indoors. Our Home Nursing exam is over & I got 77 marks. Mrs. Hill 82 & the three other people more, but I hear that Miss Dean is very pleased & Mrs. Hill is being measured for uniform in order to help at the Hospital.

Dorothy has been down staying in Ilfracombe with her Mother, the boys came for the half term & out here to tea on Sunday, but had to wait 2 hours on Mortehoe Stn' for the return train due at 5. 17 pm. David went to Bristol next morning for an interview with the Navy Authorities & has been accepted & given a badge, he passed the School Cert. but must try again for Matric. before going to University for training.

Must hurry for post. Glad you are well & getting hold of your job. Shall we see you at Easter, I suppose a lot depends on the 2nd front & transport.

With love from us both

Yours ever affect.

Mother & Father

David Jennings, grandson of Aunty Lily, and Brian's godson.

Down Top

Poole Lane

Woolacombe

N.Devon

April 22- 44

My dear Brian

First of all, thank you very much for the Penstemons which arrived from John Forbes, Hawick. They are three nice plants which I've put in the border near the path where you were digging last. I hope the slugs don't have them. We are overrun again with them. It's real growing weather, one lovely day, one rainy or misty; the slugs paradise.

We were glad that you did not stay longer at Easter, for soon after you left we had lashings of rain. Auntie & Lillian got here in the dry, but it was too wet to get primroses for Lillian to take back with her, we got her a lunch from the garden, of odds & ends.

Last Tuesday evening Daddy & I walked down to see Mrs. Lucas's garden, it is a picture with all the spring flowers, a lovely sight; they have no help at all. I don't know how she does it all for the house is beautifully kept.

Get some of the hair lotion made up, it's a pity to lose hair at your age.

I wrote to Phyllis advising her to get vaccinated & wanted to urge you all to do the same, for you are all moving about mixing with all sorts of people. You particularly give lifts to strangers, it would be wise to be done again. The case of smallpox at Combemartin turned out to be Dermatitis to everyone's relief.

Miss Dean is starting another Course of Lectures at Mortehoe, First Aid, this time. Mrs. Hill went last Thursday but very few turned up, so they hope to begin in earnest next week at 7.00pm. I couldn't go on Thursday, for Harry Ridd, his wife & mother in law came for the day & did not leave early enough. They told us that Auntie Lucy had Auntie Lorna staying there a month & Uncle Waller some of the time. We say they must be hard up for company to invite the latter.

I had 2 tiny black & cream chicks out of the hatching, poor hen looked disappointed too. One had come out of the nest & couldn't get back. 5 eggs were infertile & 4 had broken their shells & evidently hadn't the strength to come out. They were very small eggs & I believe were pullets. I shall wait for the next broody & try to get some good eggs from somewhere.

You need not write to Uncle Dick for I sent congratulations from you all - he said he only wanted our good wishes, meaning no presents; we sent £2.0.0 to buy some need for the kitchen I suggested. Have not heard yet.

Am glad that Grace Potter has recovered & hope that this will be the beginning of better health or should I say perfect. Remember me to them when you go.

Bobby has written, & Phyllis, she did not go on that Course after all & Bobby & Joan are well, but very busy, each in their own jobs.

Must hurry, have invited Miss Brown to walk down to Woolacombe this afternoon & come back to tea, a lovely day. We went to the Pictures yesterday. Mrs. Lawrence goes to

London with the boys tomorrow & Miss Brown will be tied to the house & her sister.

I have turned out the greenhouse this morning & hope to syringe it down this evening & clean it out.

With much love from Daddy & myself

Yours ever affectionately

Mother

At the top of the letter

Auntie Lily's hair restorer consists of:-

2 oz each of Rectified Spirits & Castor Oil

Shake it well together.

Auntie still uses it

Uncle Dick, Alice's brother who married later in life, in his much younger days

Undated letter. Spring 1944

My dear Brian,

Thankyou very much for all the trouble you have taken to repair the spools for my machine. I will keep them apart and then let you know how they last. It is awkward getting parts just now, but of course the machine is about one year older than you are! *(ie about 1907)* Uncle Dick offered to get it through his firm, cheaper than a Singer, & Daddy didn't then see what I wanted one for at all, we accepted Uncle Dick's offer. The needles, I'm sorry, I should have given you a sample one, I have given to Mrs. Hill as she has a Singer. We went there to tea last week & on Wed. they both came here, they are a nice couple & good to know.

Mrs. Hill & I are meeting at each other's house alternatively to practise bandaging & bed making for the Home Nursing exam, which is sometime next month.

Mrs. Hill intends to pass & then if they call her up for war work, the Red X will apply for her to help at the Hospital, she doesn't mean to help in a shop if she can avoid it.

Auntie Lily was here last weekend, she is very well.

The Aconites are coming out, & quite a few Anemones, so I actually weeded a bit yesterday opposite the kitchen & hope to do the strawberry bed as soon as I can, it's almost a lawn with that short flowering grass.

Your Chrysanthemums are still good & the Cyclamen is rapidly increasing it's blossoms. I have a shallow bowl filled with Lythospernum Polyanthus, bits of Heath etc, looks lovely. The Daphne is flowering, but is not a wonderful specimen & the pale Veronica is out, so it begins to look like Spring.

The farmer caught the last rat by putting traps under the trough, one each way & I've seen no sign since. Thank you also for the addresses. Do you think they would supply a sitting of eggs, for that is the way I would prefer to increase my brood.

We shall be interested to hear how you get on when you take up your new job. I hope you will find plenty of interest & scope for your energies & a comfortable lodging. It won't be as lonely as when you first went to Hampshire, you have made your contacts & now have people to visit weekends.

We hope you enjoyed your trip to London, & all had a good time together.

Needless to say, I've not made any more toys, I cut out 2 more pigs, but they are very fiddly things, & Matron keeps me supplied with work. I made three nightgowns last week & spent last evening cutting out more, so you see I can't afford for my machine to konk out yet awhile.

I have had a long letter from Mrs. Creighton; she asks after you all, Nurse Matthews who is 77 & Pat Ferrars, who has now left school & is studying for a Medical Course at the Chelsea Polytechnic, & Mrs. Russell, she says Alan is a Major in a crack Indian Regiment, so he has made rapid progress. I have all these to answer some time. Mrs. Hardwick enquired after all of you. Mrs. Creighton says, she still works there.

Bobby & Joan have each written & said how much they enjoyed the cockerel, so it's a relief to know that.

With love from Daddy & myself

Yours ever affectionately

Mother

Bobby says they are very busy now & on night work quite a lot but doesn't mind, he is so glad to be within easy reach of home.

Enclosed is Joan's letter, perhaps you will return when you write again.

Down Top

Wednesday 10/5/44

Dear Brian,

Mother thanks you for your letter of the 7th recd. today.

I am answering at once to let you know one or two addresses in London which we know.

Phyllis & Vera stayed at the following addresses last March.

Miss Haldane

28 Bloomsbury Street

WC1

The Ridgmount Private Hotel

65 Gower Street WC1

Bracketed Bed & Breakfast 7/6 per night

Did you know that you can stay at a Boarding House or Hotel for 4 days without a Ration Book? As they wanted to stay 5 days they had to shift after the 4th night. Just a "wangle". You had better mention Miss Vera Grant's name I think.

I stayed when last in London at

The Harlingford Private Hotel

Cartwright Gardens WC1

Very clean & nice, but nothing special about the meals.

When Mrs. Simon went to London last year she stayed at

The Bedford Hotel

Southampton Row WC1

Bed & Breakfast 10/9

(Phone Terminus 3655)

I do not think Lillian knows any addresses. She gave us The Harlingford as the only place she knew. Her address is as follows:-

Miss Watkins

Charlton Hotel

Aberdeen Park

Highbury N 5

The Charlton Hotel is a residential hotel and I hardly think you would be catered for there for a night or two.

We hope you will enjoy the change.

We were very amused with Mrs. Russell's broody hen, who sits on it's drinking dish.

I am surprised that there are crowds in Bournemouth. I thought it was in the Defence area –I think it is a very nice place indeed.

We heard from Phyllis & Ronald recently. They are both well. Ronald is grieved that he hasn't met his beloved for 5 weeks. He says it strains her patience. I wonder how long it will be before you have similar symptoms.

I have been using up "Charles" red paint lately. Given the iron wheelbarrow, water barrel stand, and roller a coat, and have started on the iron windows & doors of the bungalow where rust has occurred, especially the kitchen window which you pointed out. This fine weather is ideal painting weather, but we cannot get Mr. Norman to do the outside.

We shall be glad to see you at Whitsun if you can get away.

Charles sent us 7 "Veto – mold " tomato plants recently & which are duly planted in the greenhouse. Unfortunately, the heads of two had been knocked off, but side shoots are now growing – one of which will in time become the main stem – we shall see which is the stronger shoot.

So far mother's two new chicks are well and running about very sturdily.

The Spring, so far, has been drier than usual, and we haven't had the rain which apparently other parts of the Country have been getting.

With love from us both

Your affec father

WJL

P.S.

Mother hasn't another "broody" hen, so that nothing further is doing.

Down Top

Poole Lane

Woolacombe

N.Devon

May 23- 44

My dear Brian,

Just a hurried note in answer to yours just received. We hope you have enjoyed your little break at Cheshunt & found it interesting & had comfortable quarters in London.

I was wondering if you can manage to come for Whitsun, whether you would have liked to ask Miss Butler to come with you. Daddy says the time is too short for arranging this, but I leave it to you, you may think that the holiday is too short; a long journey & expensive fare for such a short time. Anyway, you are very welcome to ask her if you want to.

Mrs. Russell has done pretty well to have five chicks, it's possibly as many as she wants. Am sorry the situation is not any easier! I have not had another broody hen so am held up, but have one with a dropped stomach, or so Swift says. I took her in to see him last Saturday, a nice brown pullet too, such a pity.

We need rain badly, but the weather seems very settled, lovely of course. Am sorry about the frost in the Russell's garden, it's very hard when crops are spoiled.

Miss Roberts has just been, says a lot of people have had spots, it's the absence of fresh fruit she says.

With much love from us both   Mother

P.T.O.

In case you can't get down here, Auntie Lily says that Methylated Spirits takes the place of rectified spirits for the hair lotion & a drop of scent. But if you are coming we will get it here & I have plenty of scent & bottles to put the lotion in.

May 23rd The Americans started their break-out from Anzio beach.

Betty (Butler) sent a postcard to Brian on 6th June 1944, and later Brian added the note D Day. In the letter of June 13th, his father makes a joke about Daisy Lea, which can be seen here as part of Brian's address.

Chesil Beach Portland 1944

Betty's postcard sent from Weymouth on D Day.

Transcript of Betty's postcard

Tuesday.

Have just been over here right on to the top of Portland & it's really beautiful. Sat on the top & wrote some letters in hopes of having some replies! This is really an apology for the confused letter I wrote last night & hope you could make it out. I couldn't think with Mrs. C waiting for me – What news! I must buy a paper as I can't hear the wireless. Hope to see you sometime at the weekend. B.

Down Top
Poole Lane
Woolacombe
N.Devon

June 13th 1944

Dear Brian,

We have just heard that Phil Hughes died last Friday in the Hampstead Hospital after an operation for kidney & bladder trouble. This was the third operation which he did not survive very long. I thought that you had better know in case you thought of calling on them in Bournemouth.

It is very sad for Mrs. Hughes who is now absolutely alone – having no near relatives.

We are much as usual. Mother has sat another broody hen on some eggs and hopes for better luck this time. We are still getting a nice number of eggs.

After a hot spell of weather around Whitsun it has been cold & showery – but rain is wanted – if it were only warmer.

I hope you are getting on better at Daisy Lea. Who is she, by the way?

The War prospects are more encouraging aren't they? We wonder if it affects you as regards Home Guard Duties. Hope you are well.

With love from us both

Your affec father WJL

June 4th Allied troops entered Rome.

June 6th D-Day. Allied forces landed in Normandy.

June 13th First V1 landed in Britain.

Brian became engaged to Betty, and received the following letter from Betty's mother.

Tel No. Burbage 55

East Wick

Wootton Rivers

Nr. Marlborough

July 4th 1944

Dear Brian,

Betty has just phoned me your news I felt I must write a line & give you our united good wishes & heartfelt congratulations. I sincerely hope you will both be very happy & we shall look forward to seeing you both here (*the*) weekend after next. I cannot say anymore, as you will know all I feel. It is very hard to part with your children (*but*) at the same time (*it*) is nice to feel they are happily "married".

I am really very busy, only felt I must send you our wishes.

With kind love from Bettys Mother & Father

Alice E. Butler.

P.S Please forgive Ernest not writing but he is off in a rush for post & has written to Betty.

Down Top

Poole Lane

Woolacombe

N.Devon

July 10 – 44

My dear Brian

Many thanks for your letter & news. Daddy & I are very pleased indeed to hear that at last you have found your Miss Right!

We shall look forward very much to meeting Betty, & perhaps the nervousness won't be hers alone. Experts in the kitchen are apt to make some of us feel a bit self conscious.

I hope we shall like one another very much & if you are going to be happy together, that is all that matters. I am thankful that you don't have many D. bugs (*Doodle bug bombs*) to contend with. Bob & Dorothy came down on Saturday & were over yesterday & seem to have had very little rest or sleep for 3 weeks. They think that Bobby's area is not as bad as theirs, but Joan must be in a bad spot. Bobby wrote some weeks ago & said that Joan was losing sleep looking after dogs & that she was very busy at Ealing also stripping? etc since then we've not heard. Phyllis writes not to worry about her, she can only travel as far as Canterbury. Ronald we've not heard from recently, he must have been having a hot time & Stephanie at Croydon, if she is still there.

Auntie is here at present. She has had a slight stroke & her Dr. sent her into Hospital for a fortnight to rest, & says she ought not to return to the Torrs, but she is determined to go back. I feel certain that Mrs. Evans does not want her back, the responsibility is too much, for Auntie only came from Hospital last week & persistently does the most unnecessary things, like stooping down to the bottom of the safe or cupboard, so that I have to be ticking her off all the time. Her speech is affected at times & the left side of her mouth. It started with her left arm.

Dorothy & Bob are having a week here & using Auntie's room at the Torrs, they wouldn't be able to get in anywhere else now & they intend to see the Dr. & have a talk with him, for they realize that we can't have Auntie (here) for long, she would make us both like herself. The Dr. came out yesterday to see her & went all over the place trying to find this lane, but he seemed charmed with the bungalow & position when he eventually got here.

We are having horribly stormy weather, wind & rain, it's more like winter again & we have had one man painting outside, for a fortnight, & he can't get on, he has been trying to paint the uprights of the fence, you remember, they are very rusty, also he is having a job to do the inside of the iron posts because of the Escallonia.

I hope Grace Potter is well now & has quite recovered from her last operation, it must be a horrible time, having so many of the (*Doodle*) bugs over, we are quite free of them so far, touch wood.

I hope you will enjoy your weekend with Betty at her home & that they will be pleased with you as a son- in- law. Dorothy is very pleased over your news & I'm sure Miss Brown will be next door. You have always found favour in her sight. How will

Daisy Lea take it, perhaps it would cheer her up to know, take her mind off other things.

Dear Brian

I am adding my congratulations to mothers. Better late than never – but not so late as Uncle Dick of which I think we told you. His marriage I mean.

As mother was so disappointed with only two chicks, she sat another hen on 13 eggs. But after 3 or 4 days she found this hen sitting on two china eggs in another nest and the real eggs quite cold. In desperation mother bought a hen with 13 day old chicks – and then, would you believe it, the original hen brought out 9 new chicks. So we now have 2 + 13 + 9 = 24 chicks. Poultry farming seems a great lottery.

So long – must catch post

Your affec father

WJL

Betty Butler – "Miss Right", September 1940, at her home, East Wick Farm, Near Wootton Rivers, Wiltshire.

Photograph by Bert Hardy, whose wife and son were evacuated to East Wick early in the War. Bert Hardy became a celebrated photographer for Picture Post Magazine.

Down Top

Thursday July 27th 44

Dear Brian

Thank you for your letter & news. We have noted the dates 11th Aug to 16th and hope the weather will be fine.

Mother is enclosing a letter to Betty as she thought you would like her to write (to) Betty personally.

Ronald's reaction to your news was :- "It looks as if he will beat me to the post".

I wonder why Mrs. Russell wants you to leave. It must be very difficult to find a place quickly but we hope you will be able to do so.

Aunt Lily is better and has returned to Ilfracombe. How long she will act with care and discretion I don't know.

Ronald is going to a camp for a holiday from Aug14 – 26 at Leominster. He is adjucant. He proposes to bring Stephanie down here some time in September if he can manage it. We do not know their exact relationship as he is not at all definite.

We heard from Bobby recently. They were well so far. The glass in the shop window in Ealing has been blown out again.

As you say Mother is poultry farming in a "big" way. We still have a good many "old" potatoes in store for feeding.

The garden is not too good. The parsnips failed entirely. Carrots will be poor. Runner beans very tardy & want a stimulant I think.

Weather very patchy. One fine day and two or three wet & so on. Cannot mow the lawn as too wet.

We are very well, hope you are too, also Betty.

With love from us both

Your affec father

WJL

P.S.

Your letters to us & Auntie Lily were all examined by Censor.

Brian and Betty engaged July 1944.

The photograph was taken at East Wick farm.

July 20th "The July Bomb Plot" – the failed attempt to kill Hitler.

Letter dated 26/9/44 Ackd (*Brian's writing -Acknowledged*)

Down Top
Poole Lane
Woolacombe
N.Devon

My dear Brian

Thankyou very much for your two letters, both of which arrived together. I am sorry to be so long in answering them but Phyllis arrived on my birthday & to cap the sequence Ronald arrived on his (*birthday*) Sept 5th but has already gone again. All these visits on top of one another, you know we expected Ronald & Stephanie today, but he had to put his holiday forward because his Senior wanted his leave next week & the Colonel said that they must both meet in the Office on Monday so that Ronald can take over.

When this happened, Ronald suggested joining Stephanie at Chepstow but there was nowhere for him to stay, until Friday when she arranged for him to stay at a Cottage over the weekend. Also Jean was staying with Stephanie until today. Ronald left here at 8.oc on Friday morning with the idea of bringing Stephanie back with him if she cared to finish her holiday here with us, but as we have heard nothing, we suppose she has made other arrangements. We thought to see Dorothy also when she came down to fix John up for school, but he has gone home instead, as all is quiet again. The boys next door suddenly hear they are to return home on Monday for school on Tuesday. It looks as if there will be a general return to London & we shall go all quiet again here. Bobby rang up one evening to say that he was home on 2 months release from the Army & he wants Joan to get away for a month in October.

Aunty Lily was here last weekend & seems a good deal better, she is having special medicine from the Doctor & sees him at intervals. He threatens her with bed if she doesn't take care. She came loaded with things which she has turned out for you & I'm thinking you will have to pick them up on your homeward way from the honeymoon. I could add to the collection in the way of handleless cups, & odd plates, so useful when everything is new & in sets.

Please thank Betty & Mrs. Butler for their very kind letters, I will write later, it all sounds perfectly delightful, & we shall look forward to this great event. I forgot to tell Betty about her lone chick, it has joined the rest, & can look after itself very well indeed, doesn't seem to look any different to me, or bigger, & still has a very raggety tail, but it can snatch its food with the best of them. Ronald on his 2 days re-arranged the fowl run again, taking down the wire near the Simons & putting the posts next their fence & so having some wire to spare, shut off a corner this end where Bob put in a gate post, removed the inner gate & put it this end, so that I can shut the cockerels up by themselves. The hurdle was leaning against some netting & blew down, killing a white chick belonging to the same hen whose chick was lost. Daddy found it dead when Ronald & I had gone to Mortehoe, I to the Lecture & he to call on some people staying there.

Mrs. Hopkins plucked it & we gave it next door, they are pleased with it, such a pity, it was the biggest of the brood. The frightened white hen has injured her leg, so is shut up, she has laid 2 eggs since & seems to be able to stand up on both legs, so I will wait & see whether she will get better.

Daddy audited my poultry book & found that from last Sept to this we have had 1500 eggs & £1 -2-9 profit. So as a hobby it pays for itself, you see.

I suppose that you & Betty are busy looking for a suitable flat. I do hope she gets the job she wants at the College.

Trust that you have now quite lost the sand rash, it's a pity that simple pleasures should have a sting, like picking blackberries, I only got a handful one evening & some very bad scratches.

With much love to you & Betty from

Mother & Daddy

August 25th Paris liberated by the Allies.

September 3rd Brussels liberated by the British 2nd Army.

September 4th Antwerp liberated by the British 2nd Army.

September 5th Ghent liberated by the Allies.

September 8th First V2 landed in Britain.

September 30th German troops surrendered in Calais.

Down Top

Poole Lane

Woolacombe

N.Devon

Oct 12th 1944

Dear Brian

Thank you for your Picture P.C. recd this morning, also for your long letter to Mother on the 15th Sept, which has remained unanswered so far.

Mother would prefer your suggestion to go with you from Salisbury by bus to Pewsey. The 10.29 am train from here is due in Salisbury at 3.10pm. I find the 12.30 is not running now. Mother would then await your arrival. I suppose it may depend on the time the bus goes, also upon when you can get away from business that day.

We are very glad you have obtained the "dream cottage" although for so short a time. Perhaps, however, the owner will allow you to continue afterwards.

I think you are wise in getting good second hand furniture instead of utility stuff in the circumstances. As regards Mother returning on the Saturday – she doesn't want to impede you in catching your train to Torquay as might easily happen. She thinks therefore of catching the 4.45pm from Salisbury if there is a suitable bus from Pewsey to connect with it. Also she would like a little time with Bobby whom she hasn't seen for 3 years – I understand that Bobby is coming but not Joan.

I am sorry I do not feel able to face a long journey nowadays. I have heard of so many people who have travelled to London recently in great discomfort – not able to have their seat (if they get one) and in one case couldn't even move their arms or get at their lunch. In ordinary times I should no doubt have ventured forth to give you my blessing which you have anyway.

I enclose a cheque for £25 bringing my contribution to the sum I originally intended. Uncle Herbert has recently sold some of my plots on Canvey (about £100) and I can now easily afford it, so please do not say anything more about it. Perhaps it will go towards the cost of the settee to match the chairs.

I sincerely hope that you will have fine weather for the wedding and that you & Betty have many happy years in front of you.

With love to you both Your affect father WJL

Wedding Day, October 21st 1944

Brian and Betty on their Wedding Day

outside East Wick farm, Wootton Rivers, Wiltshire.

Ronald and Brian, at Wootton Rivers Church, Wiltshire

L to R Alice Lowries (Brian's mother), Dick Butler,

Alice Butler (Betty's mother) Phyllis Lowries

The following is an extract from Brian's Memoir, which describes the day of his wedding, and where he and Betty went to live shortly afterwards.

MARRIAGE OF BRIAN LOWRIES AND BETTY BUTLER.

21st: OCTOBER 1944.

The couple met in Winchester where both were employed by Hampshire County Council in different departments of Education; Brian in Horticultural Advisory work and Betty as a lecturer in Domestic Economy, Cookery and Preservation of home grown produce in Wartime. Brian had a town environment with holiday experience of the countryside and farming relatives in Devon, while Betty had grown up on the farm and loved the Wiltshire downs and countryside. However, both enjoyed living in the country although this had to be deferred for over twenty years when living in Birmingham.
The marriage took place in the Wiltshire village of Wootton Rivers, near Marlborough, The service being held in the village church of St. Andrew's and the reception in Betty's home at East Wick Farm, Wootton Rivers.
In addition to the bride's parents, Mr.& Mrs Ernest Butler,there were present the bride's brother Dick & his wife Gaynor and family, sister Mercy with husband Tom and daughter Diana. The bridegrooms mother Alice came, but Will:felt that the journey from Devonshire was more than he could undertake. The bridegroom7s brother Ronald acted as Best Man and his sister Phyllis who was in R.A.F.Service uniform also attended with relations and close friends from both sides. Brother Bob: was unable to obtain leave from the Army to come.
The honeymoon was in Torquay, and being Wartime travel restrictions were in force,especially with regard to petrol. This meant that in order to go the 28 miles from Wootton Rivers to Salisbury station, two taxis were needed as fifteen miles was the limit permitted by car. The bridegroom's mother travelled with the couple as far as Exeter where they separated with Alice going to her home at Morthoe,Nr.Ilfracombe & Brian and Betty onto Torquay.
Finding somewhere to live was a problem in 1944. Before their marriage Brian had lived with a family and Betty in a flat, thus obtaining a house to rent was difficult. At this time Brian was working for the County War Agricultural Committee & was then based in the New Forest at Lyndhurst, Betty was teaching locally at New Milton. They heard that The Lodge to a small estate at Hordle,near the coast could be rented for a few months which was a start to their house-hunting. The estate of Arnwood and Arnwood House feature in the children's book "The Children of the New Forest" by Captain Marryat.

Betty and Brian outside their first home, Arnwood Lodge, in the New Forest, 1944, which was mentioned in Brian's account.

Down Top

Poole Lane

Woolacombe

N.Devon

November 30th 1944

Dear Brian

Mother thanks you for your long letter and for the "snaps". I am afraid that we do not think a great deal of those of ourselves. Perhaps we do not "take" well or perhaps we do not really know how we look! Those of your cottage are very charming, and we hope you will be able to have it for quite a long time.

I suppose £100 is quite good for your car. I really think that Ronald should sell his, but he simply won't hear of it. There is a talk of producing a small car for £100 after the War, as you have probably noticed in the newspapers.

The weather here for a long time has been awful and our forecourt is simply running with water which cannot get away. It is very mild however.

As regards Xmas, we expect Aunty Lily, but haven't heard from Ronald lately. We think he will probably be here. In any case I think you should stick to your present arrangements as Betty will naturally like to spend her first Xmas as a wife at home with her family. We quite understand this and in fact expected it. You both know that we shall be only too happy to have you at any time you can conveniently come, although it is a very long way to come I am afraid.

I have been looking about for some little time for my usual Diary but couldn't find it, and bought a Collins Farmers Diary as the next best. I have since come across a Diary, rather smaller, which suits me better. I am therefore enclosing the other one hoping that you can make some use of it. It has a good deal of Agricultural information which may prove useful.

My dear Brian

Thankyou very much for your letter & enclosing the snaps, we should very much like some copies of all of them, it sounds very greedy, or say three which show most of your cottage. It's pretty delightful & I don't wonder Betty fell for it. It doesn't look so very small & seems to have a nice piece of garden. As regards those snaps of ourselves, I shouldn't have any enlargements of the front door couple, but we would like a copy of each, for the bird bath one shows a nice tit on the lawn, altho' Daddy looks distinctly queer, as tho' balancing on board ship.

Tell Betty we appreciate the thoughtfulness of the offer to spare us a lonely Christmas & shall look forward to seeing you later on. I shall be able to picture the family gathering at East Wick, the lovely old house was built for such gatherings. I did so enjoy my visit there & seeing Betty's parents, & Mrs. Butler showed me all over the house, it was kind of her in the midst of so much to do. So I have pictures always with me.

When is the new arrival expected by Dick's wife, I thought before Christmas.

Now that you know what Tatters (*Betty's dog before marriage, left behind at East Wick. The dog had a difficult temperament, turned on the new baby & was shot by Dick*) thinks of new comers to his home, I suppose you can arrange that they don't meet when you go home. I am glad Bobbie (*known as Bobbie dog – a stray taken in, at one point by the police – hence Bobbie - with a tendency to wander off. He was known to howl outside houses where a death was expected, so his appearance was not appreciated !)* is none the worse & showed his mettle.

Mr. Hill brings his Jill here & Susie (*Alice's dog*) & she take no notice of each other, they had their scraps in the early days of their acquaintance, but seem to tolerate each other now. I am thankful, for fights scare me.

My fowls are looking better since they have the run of the garden, they don't stand about in the wet & mud as they did. I gave Dorothy 2 very small pullets & Mr. Parker, the grocer, a cockerel to fatten up with 2 others he had bought. So those 2 people have had their Christmas presents.

Lillian had a surprise recently, her Auntie Annie left her £20, so she nearly had a fit. I hope she will straighten her affairs, they are usually in a hopeless state.

Poor David is in quarantine with mumps, in the middle of his Course at Glasgow Univ. Auntie Lily goes to the Rotunda on Saturday until March 1st, after that they put up the charges. The new Matron at the Nursery does not seem to need my services, so I am busy making large size pyjamas for the Red Cross, they are very hard up for workers with machines, so I spend the long evenings. Miss Brown is doing the button holes quite expertly. I failed that exam on the paper, it was on the Wed eve before your wedding & I felt I hadn't time for it. Miss Dean was very disappointed as I passed the Aural & Practical. All our love to you both & hope all goes well at the Office.

(*Over page*)

This has been no gardening weather anywhere recently. I should think Mr. Dadds has not been for 2 weeks.

Harry Watkins is in London taking a nine weeks Course in languages & Betty is with him, his future job will be in occupied Germany, he has just returned from a three weeks Course on something or other at Worthing.

Once again our love to Betty & yourself, so glad all the house is finished now & you can look round with pride & enjoy it.

Yours affectionately

Mother

"The front door couple".

Will and Alice outside the porch of their bungalow at Mortehoe 1944

Down Top

Poole Lane

Woolacombe

N.Devon

Dec. 20- 44

My dear Betty & Brian

What you must think of me I don't know so long in thanking you for your parcel & lovely letter, you are very sweet to your in – laws Betty & so thoughtful. Phyllis has been home for a week & only went yesterday morning, & this is the first letter I have written, nor have I sent one card, I feel too tired in the evening.

I am sorry that the gloves are <u>very</u> narrow for me, what a pity, they are beautifully made. Please don't buy me anything, you are sending us copies of the snaps, & we shall appreciate an enlargement (in spite of what Father says) & that will be present enough. Our remarks about enlargements means that they accentuate the faults & we want to pass ourselves off as better looking than we are, do you see?

I found the enclosed spoons in a drawer & thought you might like them if you have not any. I shall send this to East Wick, for fear your postmen will have to carry it to & forth while you are away.

We are in the throes! Last Sunday morn I had a telephone message to say that Auntie Lily was behaving very peculiarly & thought I had better go to see her, which I did in the afternoon. They have started buses again on Sunday afternoons, so I went by bus. I found her trying to do her hair ready for tea, it was so entangled that I cut lumps off, she had been out in the morning with (a) shoe lace untied & her knickers showing. I left her at the Hotel & asked them to call the Doctor next day. He rang me & said that she had better come here, she was incapable of looking after herself. So I took a taxi in on Monday & brought her back & have kept her in bed. You can imagine what a handful she is, her left hand is almost useless, she drops everything, & at times is very confused. A friend is bringing along a trained nurse to see me this afternoon, she has recently married again & not young & the bride- groom, nearly 70 does not wish her to go out, but we shall see, perhaps she will give me a little time occasionally, so that I can get into Ilfracombe for shopping, & then we must try to find somewhere for Auntie to go & be looked after. The Doctor promised to come out to see Auntie this week, but there is no doubt that it is another slight stroke. She has oceans of stuff at the Hotel & that will have to be fetched away for it's quite obvious that she can't go back there.

Poor Ronald is coming down to a cheery house- hold.

I do hope that you will find Mother & Father well when you go home & have a very happy time & trust the new arrival will come safely for both (*Dick & Daid Butler*) & in time for Father Christmas.

With much love to you & Brian & so glad the Bobby dog is turning out so nicely.

Yours

Mother – in – law

Bobby dog and Brian

This Wartime Christmas Card, featuring photographs of themselves, was sent by Betty and Brian to his parents.

Front page of wartime Christmas card 1944

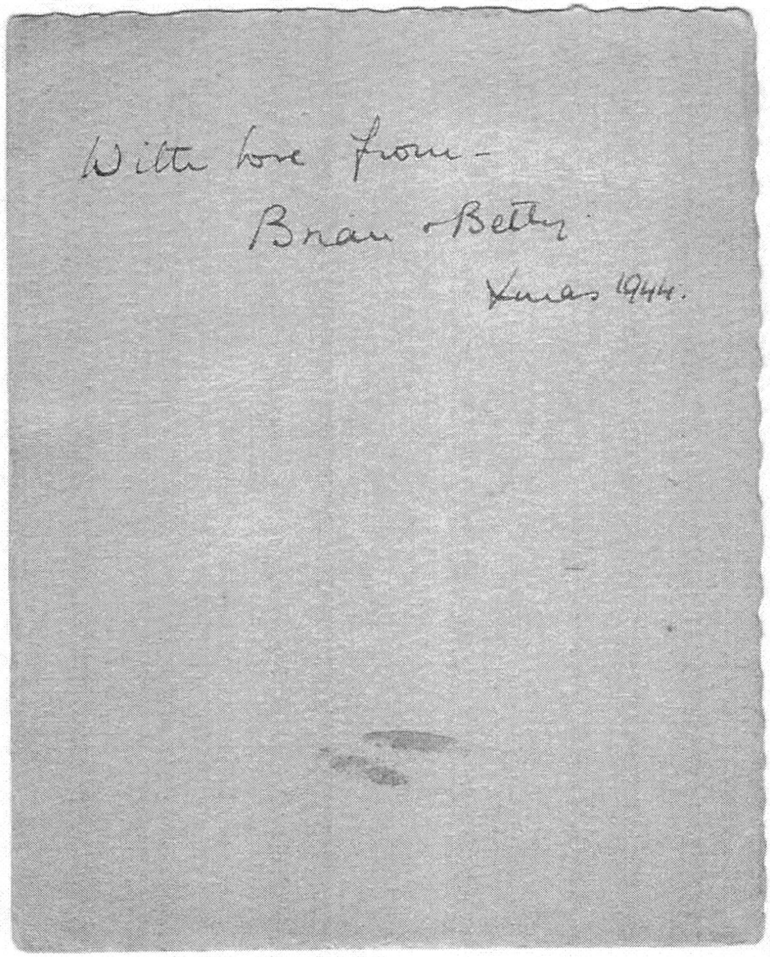

1944 Christmas Card

1945

Down Top

Woolacombe

Friday 12/1/45

Dear Brian

Thank you very much for your letter enclosing an enlargement of the photo of ourselves and for the magazines, also your previous letter & Betty's which we have been going to answer every day.

This Impetigo business is "sure" a very nasty experience and no doubt with whiskers & pink stain you do look a "tough". When you married Betty took you for "better or worse" and this is some of the worse!

Seriously, we do hope you both will soon get clear of it. It is very good of neighbours to get your things in for you.

Auntie Lily is about the same, rather improved if anything. Harry rang up one day (he is on leave after undergoing an operation for hernia) to say that he is taking charge of his mother – he's seen the Dr. and is trying to find a nursing home for her. We are very glad as Dorothy cannot do anything to help, as she went into hospital on Monday for several weeks treatment for neuritis or arthritis. It is a rather painful treatment by injections. Dorothy complains about the War tension caused by V1 & V2 bombs* dropping all around generally without any alert. No doubt this has a lot to do with her complaint.

Young John Jennings hurt his knee this Xmas – falling on the ice, and hops about with the aid of sticks.

We are using the Calender, which we did recognise as a photo of your cottage.

We haven't heard from Bobby since Xmas, but have had letters from Ronald & Phyllis. No particular news however. Ronald was going to see Stephanie's mother in London shortly, and was rather fearing the ordeal! Phyllis' letter was all about her fellow workers etc. as usual.

We are keeping pretty well, this cold weather. Hoping you will both be normal shortly.

Your affec father

WJL

**Between 8000 to 9000 V1s were launched against southern England, primarily London. Many were intercepted; up to 50 per cent by anti- aircraft fire, and by aircraft tipping the wing of the device. The V2 was a rocket which travelled so fast it was invisible. About 1000 were launched before the launching sites were overrun by the Allies.*

P.T.O.

P.S.

I enclose a letter from Kathleen Hemmings & Uncle Ernest also a cheque which I have not acknowledged.

Mother wrote sending a doll which Phyllis made when she was here, and giving news of the family including your marriage.

WJL

Letter from Kathleen Hemmings

8. 1. 45

Greenfields

Broadhidle Heath St.

My dear Auntie Alice,

Thankyou so much for your parcel & letter.

Jill's dollie, now named "Susan" is most handsome – please congratulate Phyllis on her efforts when next you write.

We were delighted to hear that Brian had married & I am sure you & Uncle must be very pleased to have another daughter – in – law. Will you kindly send them the enclosed cheque with our love & very best wishes. I trust that they will never have to be parted as most young couples today. I can say from bitter experience that it's a rotten business.

You must have had a trying time with Lily. I hope that by this time she is well on the road to recovery.

Our boys are still safe & well but it rather seems that Peter's unit is in action as we have only had freed cards since 19th Dec.

Please excuse a short note as bed, & a little need is calling!

With best wishes for 1945 to you & Uncle

Yours affectionately

Kathleen

Kathleen Hemmings (Alice's niece) and Jill

Down Top

Poole Lane

Woolacombe

Feby 23rd 1945

Dear Brian & Betty

We thank you both very much for your letters to mother recently.

We were so sorry to hear of Brian's cold and do hope it has now quite gone.

We appear to have had much more snow than you had. I measured it, with Mrs. Simon, and it was generally 18" (*inches*) deep with drifts up to 5'.0" & 6'.0". I dug a path, through 12" of snow up to the front gate on the Thursday and again on Saturday only to find that we couldn't open the gate or use the Lane owing to deep drifts. We had no post, and no tradesmen called from the Friday until the following Thursday. The main road from the station to Mortehoe was impassable with vans & carts, including our Grocer's van "snowed up". Sandy Lane was impassable even on the following Saturday (over a week).

We are glad that Betty is looking forward to a part- time job, although it will tie her down somewhat; but it will make a change I expect.

As regards Auntie Lily – Harry has now taken her to his own home near Bideford. Infact she has been there nearly 3 weeks now. Harry is back in London, but his wife is looking after the invalid with the help of a trained nurse – for how long we do not know!

I am pretty well, considering; but mother has been suffering from a nasty form of indigestion with pains in the chest & back, which doesn't seem very amenable to remedies which she has tried. I think she will have to consult a Dr. before she is really better – as she may need a special diet and treatment.

We shall be very pleased to see you both at Easter, providing mother is better – and as there are many weeks yet to go, we hope she will be by then. As regards your dog – we think Susie will be alright but what about "Pushkin", who is not very likely to be friendly – I fear. Does your dog chase cats at all?

What a nuisance the burst pipes at East Wick must have been. There was a lot of damage done in this neighbourhood, but we didn't suffer except from the water in our drive, which <u>wouldn't</u> go away – and a few "frosted" potatoes.

With love from us both

Your affec father,

WJL

Down Top

Poole Lane

Woolacombe

N.Devon

April 27th 1945

Dear Brian & Betty

Many thanks for your letters received this week.

We are glad you have been able to have several excursions to the seaside in the wonderful weather we had. It is now much colder here, but, so far, no early morning frosts; and the fruit trees look very pretty.

I have been thinking about your proposed move – but no doubt any observations on my part will be too late as you will probably have had to make a decision before you get this. Of course, if the owner of your cottage intends to increase the rent to 30/- per week as you said, which is £78 per annum – the house with bathroom, lavatory basins etc is worth £50 to you. No doubt you could sublet it – if you had to move, but you must see that there is no stipulation in the agreement to prevent sub- letting – as there sometimes is.

Phyllis was here for about 9 days including two Sundays, and the weather was very good. Unfortunately, just before she left she caught cold, although it seemed better on the morning she left. We think it is caused by the change from the heavy uniform to the thinner "civies" she always wears down here. She complains that she nearly always catches cold when here on leave, and I think the cause is the same.

We recently heard from Bobby. He is billeted in a School near Brussels which he says is a wonderful City, and has lots of facilities for Allied Forces including clubs & canteens. He says the people are very friendly and cultivate every foot of spare ground, which seems very fertile and easy to dig.

Mother thanks Betty for the recipes and the envelope with the message from Iris.

The hens are still laying very well. Mother had a broody hen, so bought 12 day old pullet chicks at 3/- each, and put under her. They sent 13 – but the hen sat on one – and later on another, (*presumably broke them*) so now they are 11. How careless of her!

Mother seems much better now and is not seeing the Dr. until the middle of next month. I have had a slight chill, but am now better. I find the changing weather trying.

With love

Your affec father

WJL

P.S.

Bobby's address

1696736 Pte Lowries R.J.

War Dogs Training School

B.L.A.

Uncle Herbert *(WJLs brother*) is seriously ill with pneumonia we heard last week, but haven't had any news this week.

Dear Both

I have been making the biscuits from your recipes, not so professional as yours, but smell good. Miss Brown has taken a sample for her tea. We have been down to the farm to fetch Ruth Hopkins, aged 4 weeks, & she is in her pram in the hall, whilst her mother goes to the dentist. They insisted on all her teeth coming out before baby was born, now she wants to get her dentures. Granny has been staying with her until now, so we may often become the nursery when she wants to go shopping etc. It's such a hill to push a pram up & so stony.

I am sorry that after making the cottage look so attractive you will have to leave it, but you certainly would find it more & more inconvenient without a bathroom, & you will make the house look equally nice. I do hope you can have it.

It is all very unsettling for you.

With much love & hoping all are well at Eastwick

Yours ever affectionately

Mother

Bobby at the War Dogs Training School, Brussels.

March 29th Last bomb fell on Britain.

Down Top

Poole Lane

Woolacombe

N.Devon

May 29th 1945

Dear Brian & Betty

Many thanks for your letters at Whitsun. Glad you had a nice time at Eastwick.

We were alone and didn't do anything very special – Ronald spent the holiday with his friend "Charles" at Worthing. Ronald tells us that he is afraid that his friendship with Stephanie will not develop into anything closer. She does not appear greatly interested in him, and as her health is not good, perhaps it is for the best. He is very unlucky in his romances. Such is life, however.

Phyllis is still at Cullen, but apparently anticipates being moved at any time. She is sending parcels of clothing & books etc as a preliminary to leaving.

Bobby is still in Belgium and I am enclosing a recent letter from him.

We are glad that the owner of the house you are after has definitely promised it to you, but there still are difficulties to overcome I see. Do you like the name "Villino"? Can't say that I do.

The only celebrations locally on V Day (*Victory in Europe Day*) that I know of, were that Mr. Simon (next door) hung out several flags and there was a bonfire & some fireworks down at Woolacombe one evening.

As regards Uncle Herbert, I understand that he is much better and is being nursed at home by Auntie May.

I quite agree about Russia. She intends to have her own way in many things, and no-one is in a position to prevent it, unfortunately.

As regards the General Election I think that the Conservatives will be returned to power, but with a reduced majority, but large enough to carry on I hope. I think that the Labour Party might have carried on the National Government until the Japs were finished as Churchill wished – and most people seem to think so too! (*Wartime coalition Government of Conservative & Labour Party*)

The garden is looking fairly well, runner beans & marrows up. Plenty of gooseberries, but not many black currants – the early potatoes escaped the frosts this year, although they were very forward.

I enclose an article by Percy Izzard about hoeing for soil moisture conservation. It quite accords with my ideas although I am not a gardener. It always seemed to me that in hot weather to disturb the soil you bring the moist portions to the surface to be burnt up like the remainder. I am a great believer with the water can – and in very dry weather water everything I have time to do. I think it is all rot about bringing the roots to the surface. As a matter of fact there seem to be many injunctions in gardening books founded on hearsay & without any scientific foundation – and these are reported from month to month for all time. Common sense & experience are the real guides I think.

It is nice to think that the basic allowance of petrol being restored will allow you to go about a bit more by car, even as far as here.

Ronald's friend "Charles" has sent us 8 tomato plants, not Vetomold this time, but a different kind, he says. They are a bit late, only arriving a few days ago, but Charles says we had some bad luck with "damping off". I suppose as we had whitefly rather badly last year, we ought to clean the canes with some kind of insecticide? before using them again.

Well, I think I have given all the news for the present. Hoping you are both well.

With love from both

Your affec father

WJL

P.S.

Mother intended to write a few words but has been busy all the morning preparing things so that she can go down to Woolacombe with Miss Brown this afternoon. I know you will understand.

May 7th Germany surrendered unconditionally

May 8th Victory in Europe (VE) Day.

Down Top

Poole Lane

Woolacombe

N.Devon

July 3rd 1945

Dear Brian & Betty

Many thanks for your two joint letters (June 22nd & July 1st) with all the latest news.

It is quite a nuisance about the workman requiring the cottage, and I agree that you should "sit tight" until you are able to obtain possession of the house.

As regards the fuel for the Domestic boiler, we used to use a mixture of small coke & anthracite – but now use only small anthracite by itself. The large anthracite is no good as it will not burn. There are kinds called "beans" and "peas" – one was too small & one just right, but our coal merchant seems to be a bit of a muddler and isn't too sure of names. Anyway, most coal merchants will know what you want for a small domestic boiler, but large stuff isn't any good at all. We have had Phurnod (PHURNOD) a prepared fuel of nice size with good results, but just recently only anthracite.

We hope you will enjoy the Conference & lectures at Long Ashton which, as you say, should be interesting.

Auntie Lily has left Harry's place quite recently and is now in a Nursing Home in S. Croydon – was driven by Betty all the way from Bideford – Her address is

Birdhurst Rise

Nursing Home

S. Croydon

Surrey

Betty thinks that Auntie is not improving – spends most of her time now in bed.

Phyllis was here last weekend. She is stationed at Portland – over 100 miles away, but got here to tea on Saturday and left after lunch on Sunday – journeyed partly by bus & partly by train. Her new address is

S/O Lowries WAAF

Royal Air Force

West Cliffe

Portland

Dorset

As regards the Election – the Ideal Government is usually considered to be one, where a strong opposition keeps the party in power up to it's election promises. Anyway, I think that as Churchill has been such a magnificent War leader he should be re-elected *to go on with the War against Japan – and I find many people also think so. I agree that Churchill's broadcasts have been rather disappointing, and Lady Bonham Carter's one of the best. The essential difference between the Liberals & the Conservatives hasn't been brought to the front at this election – but it remains. It is :- Free trade, or Tariffs against foreign goods which undercut our producers and manufacturers, or cheap foreign goods for the people and bankrupt industries in this country. We cannot compete with Russian wheat & potatoes and Japanese underwear etc: made by people with a lower standard of living than our people. The Liberals at this Election have "glossed over" this difference on their policy, which is as unfair as anything done by the other parties. (*This view expressed the state of affairs of world trade in the 1930s. By 1945, this issue was probably not raised politically, as Russia and Japan were not in a position to export anything)*

The weather has been very similar here – and today it is raining. People say "what a wretched summer" – forgetting that summer doesn't start until June 21st and that we have July, August & September to come.

With love from yours affectionately

WJL

**The General Election was held on 5th July 1945. Churchill lost to a Labour landslide victory .*

My dear Betty

It was silly of me to send the woolly, it must have been such a disappointing parcel to have something you can't wear. At the time I was stumped for ideas, Ronald & Phyllis were here & my mind principally occupied with meals. I did ask Phyllis to try & get you some stockings in Ilfracombe, but there were no fully fashioned ** ones to be had. Please accept the enclosed book of stamps, you write lots of letters & lovely long ones to us, & we do appreciate them & all your news. (*Betty's birthday was 23rd June*)

I can imagine your mother must have enjoyed her day with you & seeing all your home, it makes all the difference being able to use the car as far as the petrol will go.

I hope too that you have nice weather whilst Mercy & Diana (*Betty's sister & niece*) are with you & Brian for his trip to Bristol.

Auntie Lily writes from the Nursing Home asking me to give you two blue bed- spreads from her things here, they are blue silk, also her card table which she thinks might be useful to you. Shall I send the bed-spreads & leave the table for you to collect when next you come or let me know what you think when next you write. Spreads are for twin beds.

I am minding baby Ruth Hopkins this afternoon so that her mother can go to Woolacombe, baby is 3 months old, she is a sweet thing with a lovely smile like a little doll, very pale still & tiny, her pram is on the verandah, (sic) but it's raining again. She spends too much time in their warm kitchen I expect during this uncertain weather.

We have had a lovely lot of gooseberries & quite a few strawberries, but the slugs have been helping themselves, there are some good raspberries, but not as many as last year. I asked your picture man one day when Phyllis was in there, whether you had received your pictures safely & he said that he had been ill & so unable to send you the refund on packing case & the job description which he had forgotten to paste on the back. He said he had a letter to you half written. I had always forgotten to ask you about this. Hope you have now heard from him.

We have not yet been offered a lift to Mortehoe where we have to vote, so I hope the weather will clear up for that day or many people will fail to turn out.

With much love from us both to you & Brian hoping that you both keep well, remembering us kindly to all your family.

Yours very affectionately   M. in law

***With the invention of nylon, fully fashioned stockings with a seam down the back were extremely popular in the 1940s.During wartime they were not readily available, and some women drew a seam on their legs to imitate the real thing.*

Down Top

Poole Lane

Woolacombe

N.Devon

Saty Sept 15th 1945

Dear Brian & Betty

We were glad to hear through Ronald that you had purchased new tyres for the car & that with a new battery the car was going well.

Brian and Betty's Ford 10 car, near St. Austell, Cornwall, August 1945.

Betty wrote on the back of the photograph that they were packed up, and on their way to visit them.

The day after you left, Ronald's car came back looking so clean & smart but running on the old battery notwithstanding that old Simpson had said a new one would be necessary & would put one aside. As we expected Ronald on the Wednesday (the 5th, his birthday) we tested the battery on the Sunday and the lights & the horn wouldn't act, so on Monday, I asked Mr. Simpson what he intended to do. He first said he hadn't got a new battery, but later in the day said he had got a new one & would put it on charge but it wouldn't be ready until Thursday afternoon. In the meantime Ronald had postponed his birthday until last Monday. In the end the new battery didn't arrive until a short time before Ronald arrived on Monday afternoon – but he was able to go for his luggage after tea.

We like Dorothy – very natural, but oh so young. She simply trips up & down stairs like a fairy although she is substantial. Ronald, of course, still looks very young so I suppose it doesn't matter. The weather has been very poor – lots of rain but the couple have been out a great deal – to Mortehoe & Woolacombe. Yesterday they went to Barnstaple for the day which was very wet, and on to Bideford where they bought a bedstead and brought it back – part on the back of the car & part inside.

They went off this morning soon after 9 o clock for their 240 mile journey to Maidstone, luckily it was fine.

We have just received a wire from Bobby saying that he is home on leave and that he & Joan are coming here tomorrow (Sunday) until Thursday. I haven't seen Bobby for 4 years & Joan for over 5 years.

Phyllis was on a 3 weeks course at Preston Lanes – but we think she must be back at Portland by now but are not sure. (Have just heard that Phyllis is at Sidmouth Devon)

The weather has been miserable and I haven't been able to mow the grass for some time. Had some nice runner beans, but I fear that the cold weather may finish them. A nice lot of tomatoes, but no sun to ripen them. I understand that the harvest in the south is rather poor, but very good in the north where they have had a fine summer. Perhaps it will be our turn next year.

Mother wishes Betty to know that the fly papers are very effective and we are very thankful. Horrid things flies!

We hope you both are keeping well. No more colds. We are fairly well mother feeling tired which is natural I suppose.

With love from us both to you both

Your affec father WJL

I thought you would both be interested to know a little more about your future sister – in – law. She is an attractive little thing, dark hair, wears glasses with pale rims (I wonder if Bettys are to be like them, the new ones) a very firm chin! Like Nursie Matthews? She has a bed sitting room with a single lady, & has to cook & do everything for herself, she has the use of the kitchen for cooking her meal on Sundays, weekdays she has Hospital dinners, not too good. Dorothy is therefore not quite a novice at house keeping, she is practical & I think Ronald is fortunate.

It is quite exciting having Bobby & Joan so much sooner than we thought, wish you could have met them. Hope the house is getting ready for you. Much love M.

P.S. The Dr. has discharged me, a great relief.

Ronald and Dorothy's marriage after the War November 1947

August 6th First atomic bomb dropped on Hiroshima

August 9th Second atomic bomb dropped on Nagasaki

September 2nd Japan surrendered

Down Top

Poole lane

Woolacombe

N.Devon

Oct 1st 1945

Dear Brian & Betty

Thank you for your print letter about a fortnight ago.

Bobby & Joan came by car on Sunday (the 16th Sept) and left on the following Thursday about 3. 0 clock and arrived home about 9.30 pm. Phyllis also came on that Sunday for 48 hrs. On the Sunday they all (except myself) went to Dartmoor and took their lunch with them. It was a glorious day when they started, but at midday there was a very sudden storm and I am afraid the party got a bit wet. After tea Phyllis left Okehampton by train for Sidmouth where she is now stationed.

Joan looked very tired when they arrived on the Sunday (about 9.30 pm) but looked much better when they left. Bobby went back to Belgium last Thursday evening. He is hoping to get an early release under the new regulation applying to owners of "one man" businesses.

Ronald left the War Office last Saturday and is now at his old address in Worthing and is with his old firm "Robinson & Rood". He & Dorothy had a good journey home from here – they left soon after 9 am & arrived at Maidstone about 9.20 pm, doing about 255 miles. Very tiring driving all that way, as Ronald admitted. Nothing is yet decided about the wedding so far as we know. It probably depends, as you said, on finding a suitable house.

Mother met Phyllis in Exeter last Friday and they had a good "look around".

Dorothy Jennings & Bob have just had a holiday at Margate and Dorothy is writing again with her right hand so is evidently better.

We are sorry you have been troubled with fleas and hope the trouble is now over. We haven't had this complaint, but Susie (*dog*) was swarming with them, hundreds – mother has taken the matter in hand, but I don't think it is over yet.

The weather has improved lately. Perhaps, as you say, we shall have a nice Autumn. It would help to shorten the winter. We are still picking runner beans. We have had several marrows, but nothing like what we would expect from 9 plants all apparently "going strong". I'm afraid that gardening like farming is a very "chancy" affair.

We are both pretty well, and hope you are also

With love

Your affec father

WJL

P.S. Our wireless is back, but after two days went wrong again. We bought a new "cheap" set (about 12 guineas) and it is "going strong" so far!

My dear Both

Very many thanks for both your letters. I seem not to have written to anybody for ages, but Bobby & Joan arrived almost on top of Ronald & Dorothy; next day, in fact so it was one excitement after another. Bobby stopped his car at the top of our lane & decided it was too narrow & not the one he was looking for & so found himself down in the Village, it was quite dark, past 9 o clock when they arrived, otherwise no doubt he would have recognised the lane again. It is 5 ½ years since he drove us down. Bobby looks very well & broader in the shoulders I think.

I feel very sorry about the flea complex, it becomes an obsession if a cure is not forth coming. Auntie Lily used Kurmarge for her dogs years ago. It's a dark brown powder & I feel sure it was very efficacious? spelling. Of course you may not be able to get it now, but I should have a good try for it. Fortunately Susie keeps hers to herself, the fleas I mean. The day you left I combed her & found a lot so bathed her & then had no time until last week when the same process I put her thro' but with some carbolic in the water, when she was dry I combed her again & found a lot more, still alive, poor Susie hates this concentrated attention but I tell her Ladies do not have fleas. I shall try to keep the treatment going, tho' not the bath. I smothered her in Pulvex which Joan thinks is good, but I've seen her scratching since.

Did you hear that Ronald's car on the home-ward journey behaved like a perfect lady, the distance was 255 miles, I wonder if they took the coast road, they talked of doing so. We phoned Simpson & got him to send up a new battery the afternoon Ronald arrived, so they walked from the Station in pouring rain, dripping off their noses (I believe you did the same once) but were able to drive to the Stn later & collect their luggage. You would have enjoyed seeing them depart. They went to Bideford the day before & returned with a single bed tied on the back & soaring in the air, held in place by torn shreds of mattress cover, one piece from end to end of car fastened to the bonnet, for all the World like a celebration of some sort. It was a very nice bed, the fellow one had been sold the previous day. I seem to be repeating the same things so had better stop, trusting you got the better of the plague & have no bites where they show, so difficult to explain!

Our tomatoes are ripening slowly & are very good, remember us to the parents at Eastwick hoping they & the families are well. With very much love & hope you both keep well & will soon get into your house.

Have you heard anymore as to your future jobs. You will be leaving soon Betty I expect & be very glad, no doubt; there will be lots to do preparing to move again. Can you secure any coal?

We have been saying no end of things about our coal merchant; but today with all the clothes in the garden, he arrives, with 5 cwt of coal. Fortunately the clothes were dry & I soon removed them, no anthracite yet. I hope you will be able to get some coal in when you want it. You can't very well whilst the nuns are there I suppose.

Phyllis now thinks she may have to stay on until the Spring, but she is making enquiries in Exeter about attending some life classes & getting some regular practise once again. (*Phyllis had studied Art before the War*)

Goodbye A.U.L.

The Brig. has sold his house & bought one near Tiverton - Aunty Lily gives us the news.

Joan, (Bobby's wife) Phyllis and Alice (letter writer) on Woolacombe sands after the War about 1948

Down Top

Poole lane

Woolacombe

N.Devon

October 25th 1945

Dear Brian & Betty

Thank you Brian for your letter of the 14th Inst and Betty for her letter to mother on the 19th.

We are very glad that Mr. Butler (*Betty's father*) has so far recovered from his severe attack, and we trust that the family will be able to keep him quiet, so that he benefits from the care & skill of his Dr. I am a "nice one" to say this as I am afraid I do not do as the Dr. advises but I know I am better if I do so.

We hope you will be able to get into your new house next week and will find it more comfortable & convenient, but moving is a terrible business I always think - and I don't suppose you like it anyway. There seem to be some people who love moving. A man once told us that a "move"gave his wife a new lease of life!

However, we have been feeling lately that a little change would be beneficial and have decided to go to Torquay on Tuesday 30th for a fortnight. We shall be staying at the Howden Court Private Hotel Croft Road, so far as we know, as they have accepted us for that time. Although mother is out of the Dr's hands she has a return of the old symptoms now & again and a change from the household "grind" is really necessary. Although we haven't suffered from bombing during the War, we have felt with everyone else restrictions especially in regard to rationing etc.

The weather is now very wild & wet after a very nice warm spell. However, we are hopeful that it will soon change again.

Ronald sent us some "Bramleys" through a friend at Faversham, Kent. Very nice indeed! Ronald has settled down at Worthing in his "old office" & is staying at his old address (49 Sheridan Road). He cannot find a house in Worthing so he hasn't been able to do anything about the wedding, and he is working late at the office as they are so busy.

Phyllis is still at Sidmouth, but as she & another WAAF have had a row with the CO. she doesn't know if she will be transferred to another station or slung out of the Service. She refers to the incident as a "Volcanic Eruption". It seems a pity I think. When I was an employee (for many years) I often had cause to complain, sometimes seriously, but I learnt to control myself, and was always glad afterwards.

I hope you are both well, especially Betty, after her adventure or mis-adventure.

With love

Your affec father

WJL

My dear Betty

Thank you very much for your letter, you really do say the nicest things! I am so glad to hear that the operation was successful & that you are feeling pretty fit again. I am glad you won't have to return to school again, it's too much with the move & also the anxiety over your father.

The rest is missing.

Down Top

Poole lane

Woolacombe

N.Devon

Oct 28th 1945

Dear Brian & Betty

Many thanks for your letter and kind wishes on my birthday. I heard from Ronald, Phyllis, Lillian and Auntie Lily.

We hope your move on Saturday went well and the weather better than it has been lately. It is very nice to have the decorations done before you moved in. So sorry about Brian's cold – hope it is now much better. So you didn't forget "mentholatiun" (?) after Betty's experience in the summer!

The rough weather recently doesn't appear to have done any damage to the bungalow, of course we have had the usual pools on the window cills and taking out the upstairs window to insert lead work hasn't cured the trouble as we thought it would. The storms were however rather unusual.

As you say the beans & marrows are now finished.

We are glad Mr. Butler is better.

As regards my being a grandfather – as Bobby & Joan haven't any children, and (until your marriage) – Brian & Ronald were single and my only brother hasn't any children I have long got used to thinking that the name of Lowries would die out. Do not therefore do anything rash on my behalf (joke over).

Mother is very delighted with the towels and thanks you very much for them. Have given your new address to Ronald & Phyllis.

Love from both

WJL

This is the last letter from 1945. William would no doubt have been pleased to know that by 2018, there are 6 great grandsons of his and Alice who bear the Lowries surname. There also are 19 great- great grandchildren descendants; three of whom have the Lowries surname.

On November 20th The Nuremburg War Crimes Trials began.

In December 1945 the Home Guard was disbanded.

Maps of North Devon

Location of North Devon in the UK

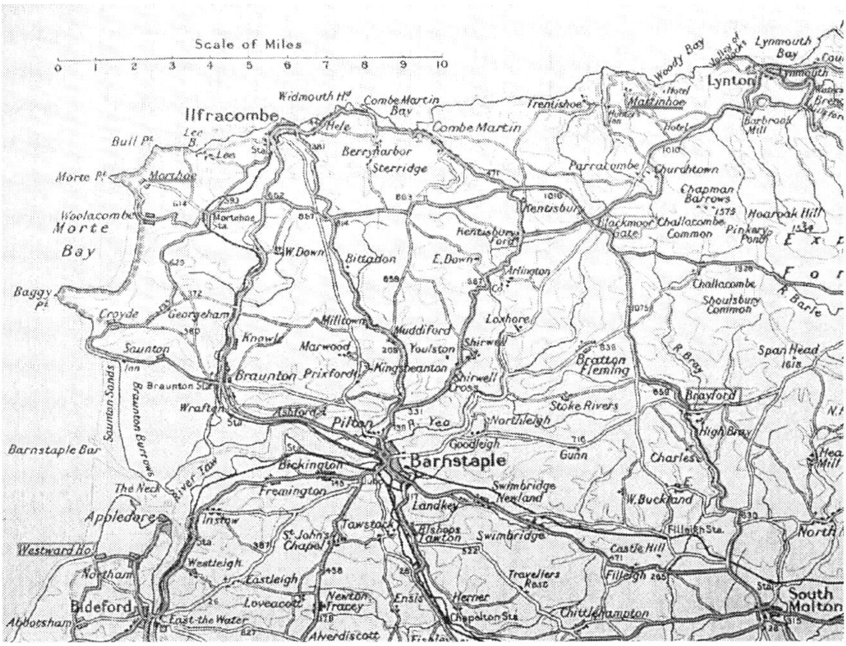

Section taken from a Bartholomew touring map of 1939

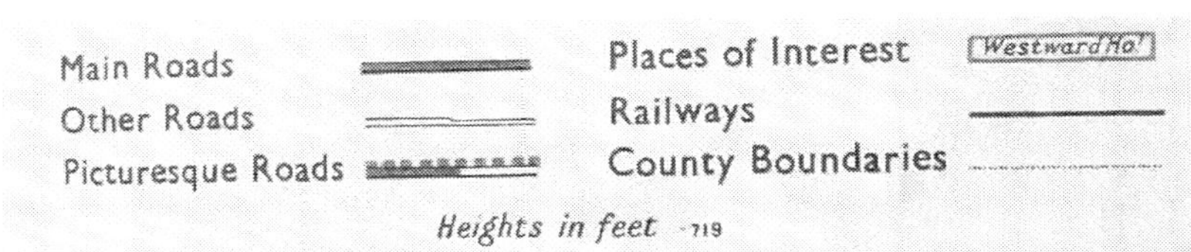

This map of 1939 shows most local places mentioned in the letters, except for Rockham Bay which was below Morte Point. Woolacombe Bay was then called Morte Bay. William and Alice lived at Morthoe, underlined, although this does not appear on their address heading. Near Lynton is Martinhoe, underlined, where Alice had lived as a girl with her mother and step-father, John Ridd.

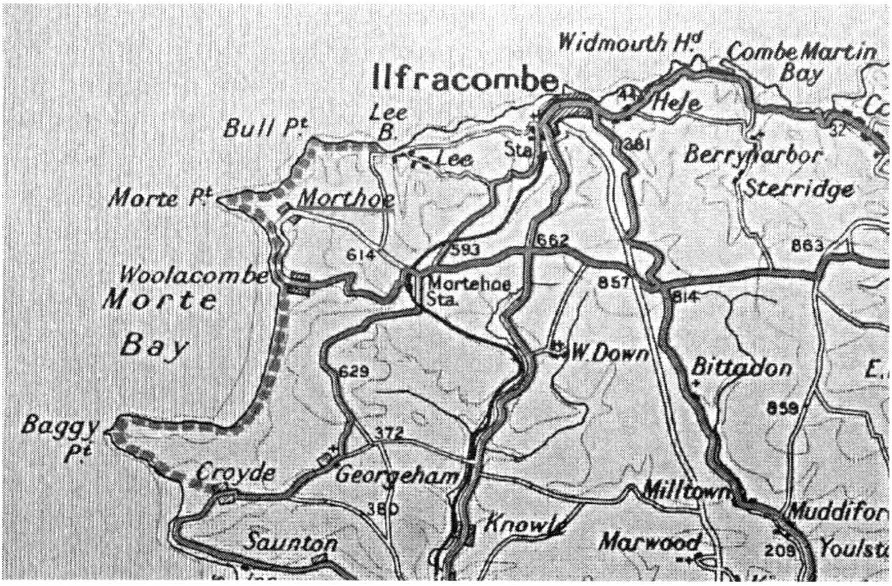

Closer section of the previous map showing the location of Mortehoe, Woolacombe, Lee, Croyde, and the station mentioned in the letters.

Family background information relating to the letters

Alice Bristow was born 26/8/1882, the 8th of 11 children, to Mary Ann and Richard Bristow.

William John Lowries was born October 1871 at Old Ford, Bethnal Green, London. He became a quantity surveyor in London, and through his friend and fellow quantity surveyor, Ben Bristow met Ben's sister, Alice. She had left her home in Devon for London, and worked as a milliner.

On June 4th 1907 Alice and William were married at Martinoe Church, near Barnstaple, North Devon. (See last photograph in this section)

Alice and William had four children, three sons and one daughter; Brian born 11/08/1908, Ronald born 5/9/1910, Robert (Bobby) born 9/1/1913 and Phyllis born 3/10/1917.

"Aunty Lily" was born 24/7/1869. She was Alice's eldest sister and the closest and most frequent visitor to "Down top".

Aunty Lily married Watkins, a solicitor, and had three children:- Lillian, Dorothy, and Harry. Lillian was unmarried, Dorothy married Robert Jennings and had sons David and John. Brian was David's god father. Harry Watkins was Aunty Lily's son who is mentioned in the letters.

On the day of Lily's wedding, 13th August 1892, her father, Richard Bristow died. The wedding went ahead and her mother Mary Ann was supported by a cousin of Richard's, John Philip Ridd. (*Richard Bristow and John Ridd's mothers were sisters – the surname was either Frankland or Franklyn.*) She later married him and went to live at Town Farm, Martinhoe, on the edge of Exmoor. As Alice was one of the younger children, she spent her early years there.

Mary Ann (Alice's mother) and John Philip Ridd and Lorna Ridd outside Town Farm, Martinhoe, probably 1920s.

Note: R.D. Blackmore used the name of Ridd in his novel Lorna Doone, but it is not known whether he knew the Ridd family, who came from the Exmoor area.

Another of Alice's brothers was Dick, who married Joan Tipper late in life, in 1944. (Letter April 22nd 1944) They were neighbours of Ronald and Dorothy in Worthing for many years. In 1981, Joan wrote to Brian an account her husband had told her of the traumatic events of the day of Lily's wedding. Although, not all the letter strictly relates to the Lowries family, it is interesting nevertheless, and is reproduced here in full.

15 Heather Lane

High Salvington

Worthing

BN13 3 BU

Dec 28/81

Dear Brian & Betty,

Thankyou both for your card & good wishes & for the interesting items you have found out about the Bristow family. Perhaps I can add a little more from what Dick told me – I have his Birth Certificate which says he was born at The Grove, Mount Pleasant, Hornsey, in 1879; & as your mother was younger I think, she & Lucy & John must have lived there too till their Father died. Dick always spoke as if the elder brothers were there too until I suppose they left to earn their living. I enclose a little slip which your mother sent to Dick which explains where the name Bristow originated from. They came as you will see from Bristol which in the past was called Bristow, so perhaps you might find more information from that part of England. Certainly "all ship shape & Bristol fashion"applied to Dick & to all of you too! (*In fact, Brian discovered that Richard Bristow came from a hamlet called*

Lowden, near Chippenham, Wiltshire; Mary Ann née Hatherall also came from the Chippenham area.)

Now another item. On the day your Aunty Lily was married your Grandfather (*Richard Bristow*) took his pony & trap & Dick with him in the early morning to his office in Red Lion Square, London, possibly for some business & to get money. Coming home he collapsed & fell over Dick who was only about 11 & pinned him to his seat under this heavy man. Fortunately, they were near a Pub I think & his Father taken there dead, & poor Dick freed. It was a terrible experience for him & of course for your Grandmother & Lily & family who had to be told – what a tragedy.

Your Grandfather built his house at Hornsey & developed the neighbourhood. Dick told me it was a big roomy house with a stable for the horse & trap & they had an old man to look after same. They all seemed in his recollection to have had a happy childhood there. There was a very High Church near where the boys had to be choir boys & were there nearly all Sunday, possibly to give their elders a rest! When he grew up Dick was not a fervent church goer in consequence! With such a big family (eleven I was told) your Grandfather was a busy man day & night!! & your poor Grandmother too. He had planned to build a house at Northwood & retire but died suddenly & only in his late forties.

Richard Bristow 1846 - 1892

Dick was very shaken after such an experience & so young & he was sent away & I think it was to Laycock & when the crash came they possibly all went there (I don't know for certain) till your Grandmother married Philip Ridd. Dick had to turn out early to earn what living he could at an early age. House & contents sold, but Dick determinedly kept one item. A dear little old mahogany dressing table set, bow fronted & siding hung Glass. I still have it.

I too come from old families on both sides. My Father's surname was Tipper (slightly funny & not euphonics!) but it was an old Saxon name from tipping the arrows, & such like names of Chipper who chipped stones. In later years they became Millers & Brewers. In Dicken's Martin Chuzzlewit Mrs. Gamp always kept a bottle of Tipper's Ale on the "mantleshelf where I can help meself when so disposed"! My mother was a Gomme – one of her ancestors was governess to George 3^rd^s Daughters, also an Admiral or some Architects. My Grandfather designed & carried out the Basingstoke Canal.

Old family history is most interesting & I wish I had listened more to my grandmother Gomme, whom I well remember as she died in 1920, 90 years old & was born in William 4ths reign & remembers Queen Victoria coming to the throne!

If you have any more about the Bristow family let me know. How glad I am I changed my name from Tipper to Bristow, much more elegant!

I hope you enjoyed a very Happy Christmas – I had a very pleasant afternoon & evening with Ronald & both boys & their wives & Baby Sarah & Rachel & another friend, so we were quite a crowd. Lovely weather Christmas Day in spite of heavy snow on Christmas Eve night, so it was a white Christmas. I expect you have had your share of snow & cold. Horrible! I do hope Betty keeps better.

Every good wish to you both for 1982 & love from

Joan.

Dick and Joan Bristow

Four of the Bristow brothers Dick, Edgar, Roland and Ben. It was from knowing Ben Bristow that William Lowries met Alice.

Some more family members including Aunty Lily were at Phyllis's wedding in 1952.

Aunty Lily is shown here sitting next to her sister Alice, and behind Alice is Dorothy, one of Lily's daughters.

Back row: Brian, Dorothy and Bob Jennings

Front row: Alice Lowries and Lily Watkins. (Aunty Lily)

Left to right: Probably Brian Lowries, Alice Lowries centre, Dorothy Jennings, (Aunty) Lily Watkins

At the same wedding was Aunty Lily's other daughter Lillian, sitting next to Ronald's wife, Dorothy.

Left to right: Lillian Watkins and Dorothy Lowries.

Sidney and Lucy Ridd are mentioned in Letter Oct 13th 1943. Sidney Ridd married Lucy Bristow, Alice's sister. They kept the post office at Mortehoe for some years.

Sidney and Lucy Ridd
from their wedding day photograph.

Harry Ridd is also mentioned in the above letter of Oct 13th 1943, and in the letter of April 22nd 1944.

Harry Ridd taken from Alice and Will's wedding photograph, 1907

Wedding Photograph of Alice Bristow and William Lowries

4th June 1907

Alice (front row 3rd from left) next to William in their wedding photo of 4th June 1907, outside Town Farm, Martinhoe, North Devon. This photograph shows mostly members of the Ridd family. On the far left is Mr. Webber, the best man and London business colleague of William, and on the far right is John Ridd, Alice's step- father standing next to her mother, Mary Ann Ridd.

Postscript

The Biscuit Tin contained other bundles of letters from my grandparents to my father. He had packaged them into groups from the 1950s and 60s, and collected them until my grandparents died. Alice died in 1964 and William in 1966.

Alice and William moved from Down Top on 28th July 1954 to a bungalow on the edge of Dartmoor to be near their son Bobby, and his wife Joan.

Bobby had moved to Dartmoor to be a veterinary practitioner, and to keep a dog kennels with Joan. They remained there all their lives.

Brian and Betty moved to Birmingham, where he was an Horticultural Educational Advisor. Betty taught Domestic Science for 25 years. They retired to Cambridgeshire.

Ronald and Dorothy lived in Worthing all their lives. Ronald continued his profession, which was the same as his father, of quantity surveyor.

Phyllis married Jim Brooker, a language translater, and lived in London.

William and Alice were keen to keep the family in touch. Their grandchildren still keep in contact, these days by email and sometimes social media. Occasionally they meet up on the edge of Dartmoor, near where their grandparents once lived.

23158532R00127

Printed in Great Britain
by Amazon